AMC's REAL TRAIL MEALS

Wholesome Recipes for the Backcountry

Ethan & Sarah Hipple

Appalachian Mountain Club Books
Boston, Massachusetts

AMC is a nonprofit organization, and sales of AMC Books fund our mission of protecting the Northeast outdoors. If you appreciate our efforts and would like to become a member or make a donation to AMC, visit outdoors.org, call 800-372-1758, or contact us at Appalachian Mountain Club, 10 City Square, Boston, MA 02129.

outdoors.org/publications/books

Copyright © 2017 Sarah Hipple and Ethan Hipple. All rights reserved.

Distributed by National Book Network.

Front cover: Couscous photograph by Jennifer Wehunt
Back cover: Taco photograph by Oskar Karlin, Creative Commons on Flickr
Book design by Abigail Coyle

Contains recipes abridged and adapted from Joanie Albers, Joe Roman, and AMC

Published by the Appalachian Mountain Club. No part of this publication may be reproduced or transmitted in any form or by any means, electronic or mechanical, including photocopying and recording, or by any information storage or retrieval system, except as may be expressly permitted by the 1976 Copyright Act or in writing from the publisher.

Library of Congress Cataloging-in-Publication Data
  Names: Hipple, Ethan, author. | Hipple, Sarah.
  Title: AMC's real trail meals : wholesome recipes for the backcountry / by
    Ethan and Sarah Hipple.
  Other titles: Appalachian Mountain Club's real trail meals
  Description: Boston, Massachusetts : Appalachian Mountain Club Books, 2017. |
  Identifiers: LCCN 2016055225 (print) | LCCN 2017013040 (ebook) | ISBN
    9781628420616 (ePub) | ISBN 9781628420623 (Mobi) | ISBN 9781628420609
    (pbk.)
  Subjects: LCSH: Outdoor cooking. | Backpacking--Equipment and supplies. |
    Camping--Equipment and supplies.
  Classification: LCC TX823 (ebook) | LCC TX823 .H57 2017 (print) | DDC
    641.5/78--dc23
  LC record available at https://lccn.loc.gov/2016055225

The paper used in this publication meets the minimum requirements of the American National Standard for Information Sciences-Permanence of Paper for Printed Library Materials, ANSI Z39.48-1984. ∞

Outdoor recreation activities by their very nature are potentially hazardous. This book is not a substitute for good personal judgment and training in outdoor skills. Due to changes in conditions, use of the information in this book is at the sole risk of the user. The author and the Appalachian Mountain Club assume no liability for accidents happening to, or injuries sustained by, readers who engage in the activities described in this book.

Interior pages and cover are printed on responsibly harvested paper stock certified by The Forest Stewardship Council®, an independent auditor of responsible forestry practices. Printed in the United States of America, using vegetable-based inks.

6 5 4 3 2 1   17 18 19 20 21 22

MIX
Paper from
responsible sources
FSC® C005010
www.fsc.org

CONTENTS

Acknowledgments   xi
Introduction   xii
   About Us   xiii
How to Use This Book   xv

1 • FOOD IN THE BACKCOUNTRY   1

- **NUTRITION**   1
  Daily Calorie Needs   2
  Carbohydrates   2
  Proteins   4
  Vegetables and Fruits   5
  Dairy   5
  Fats   6
- **FLAVOR**   6
- **SPECIAL DIETS**   7
  Vegetarian and Vegan   8
  Dairy Free   8
  Gluten Free   9
  Paleo, Atkins, Cleansing, and Other Weight-Loss Diets   9

2 • PLANNING YOUR TRIP   11

- **MEAL-PLANNING GRID**   11
- **YOUR BACKCOUNTRY PANTRY**   12
  Choosing Ingredients for the Backcountry   12
  Repackaging   14
  All-Purpose Mixes   16
  Dehydrated Foods   16
  Customizing for Your Own Preferences   20
  Spice Kits   21
  Condiments   21

- **YOUR BACKCOUNTRY KITCHEN** — 23
  - Essential Backcountry Kitchen Gear — 23
  - Stoves — 26
  - Measuring Cups and Spoons — 27
  - Pie Irons — 27
  - Paddling Extras — 27
- **PACKING YOUR FOOD** — 28
- **RESUPPLYING** — 29

3 • ON THE TRAIL — 33

- **CAMP KITCHEN** — 33
- **LEAVE NO TRACE** — 34
- **COOKING SAFETY IN THE BACKCOUNTRY** — 34
- **COOKING OVER FIRE** — 36
- **OTHER COOKING METHODS** — 37
  - Reflector Ovens — 38
  - Dutch Ovens — 39
  - Fry-Bake Pans — 40
  - A Note on Cooking Fish — 41
- **KEEPING FOOD SAFE FROM ANIMALS** — 41
- **WATER TREATMENT METHODS** — 43
- **DISHWASHING** — 44
- **REHYDRATION** — 45

4 • BREAKFAST — 47

- **COFFEE** — 48
- **GRANOLAS AND BREAKFAST BARS** — 50
  - Basic Granola Method — 50
  - Coconut Cashew Granola — 51
  - Cranberry Nut Granola — 52
  - Almond Sesame Mango Granola — 52
  - Pistachio Apricot Granola — 53
  - Dark Chocolate Coconut Granola — 54
  - Peanut Butter Banana Breakfast Bars — 55

- **MUFFINS**   56
  - Basic Skillet Muffin Mix and Method   56
  - Donut Skillet Muffins   58
  - Blueberry Skillet Muffins   59
  - Cranberry Orange Skillet Muffins   60
  - Morning Glory Skillet Muffins   60
- **PANCAKES**   61
  - Basic Pancake (Caker) Mix and Method   61
  - Cornbread Cakers   62
  - Homemade Syrup   62
- **EGG DISHES**   64
  - Basic Egg Scramble   64
  - Denver Scramble   66
  - Huevos Rancheros   67
  - Hash Brown and Bacon Scramble   68
  - Spinach, Mushroom, and Bacon Scramble   69
  - Breakfast Burritos   70
  - Omelet in a Bag   71
- **POTATOES AND GRAINS**   72
  - Backcountry Home Fries   72
  - Fried Bagels   73
  - Fried PB&J Pita   74
  - Tasha's Breakfast Couscous   75
  - Oatmeal   76
- **SWEET TREATS**   78
  - Dottie's Downhome Coffee Cake   78
  - Sarah's Super-Sticky Caramel Rolls   80

5 • COLD LUNCHES AND SNACKS ON THE GO   83

- **SMORGASBORD COMBOS**   84
  - Cheddar and Slivered Garlic Lunch Combo   84
  - Sardines, Avocado, and Hardtack Lunch Combo   85

- **FRUIT LEATHERS** 86
  Basic Fruit Leather Method 86
  Sweet and Spicy Mango Fruit Leather 87
  Strawberry Fruit Leather 88
  Mixed Berry Fruit Leather 88
- **JERKIES** 89
  Basic Beef Jerky Method 89
  Teriyaki Beef Jerky 90
  Honey Barbecue Beef Jerky 90
  Peppered Beef Jerky 91
  Malaysian Pork Jerky (Bak Kwa) 92
- **NUTS AND NUT BUTTERS** 93
  Sweet and Spicy Rosemary Cashews 93
  Chipotle Honey Roasted Peanuts 94
  Curried Almonds 95
  Cinnamon-Spiced Pecans 96
  Classic Good Old Raisins and Peanuts (GORP) 97
  Tropical Trail Mix 97
  Fruits and Nuts Trail Mix 98
  Cashew Butter 99
  Chocolate Hazelnut Heaven 100
- **VEGGIE NIBBLES AND SPREADS** 101
  Ants on a Log 101
  Banana Boat 102
  Peanut Butter-Filled Dates 103
  Buffalo Cauliflower "Popcorn" 104
  Hummus 105
  Edamame Herb Hummus 106
  Black Bean Spread 107
  White Bean Spread 107

- **GRANOLA BARS**   108
  Double Chocolate Granola Bars   108
  Cherry Choco-Nut Granola Bars   109
  Chocolate Peanut Butter Granola Bars   110
  Blueberry Granola Bars with Vanilla Icing   111
  Ski Bars   113

6 • HOT DINNERS AT CAMP   115

- **SAUCES AND SEASONING**   116
  Dry Alfredo Sauce   116
  Dry Marinara Sauce   117
  Dry Pesto Sauce   118
  Taco Seasoning   119
- **BREADS AND WRAPS**   120
  Ethan's Bomber Bread   120
  Cornbread   122
  Bannock   123
  Basic Pizza   125
  Basic Calzones   126
  Pozole Pie   127
  Quesadillas   128
  Burritos   130
  Cozy Pigs   131
- **PASTAS AND CASSEROLES**   132
  Gado Gado Noodles in Peanut Sauce   132
  5-Minute Gado Gado   133
  Cauliflower Pine Nut Pasta   134
  Chicken and Bacon Cheesy Pasta   136
  Tortellini Carbonara   137
  Penne with Squash, Tomatoes, and Basil   138

Mushroom Rigatoni 140

Fettuccine Alfredo 141

Gnocchi with Browned Butter and Sage 142

Pesto Pasta with Sun-Dried Tomatoes and Pine Nuts 143

Pesto Pasta with Veggies 144

Chili Mac 145

Tuna Pea Wiggle 146

Beef Stroganoff 147

Pad Thai 148

Baked Lasagna 149

Deconstructed Lasagna 151

Macaroni and Cheese 152

Buffalo Mac and Cheese 154

Bacon and Kale Mac and Cheese 154

- **SAVORY CAKES AND RICE** 155

Cheesy Potato Cakes 155

Veggie Potato Cakes 156

Sausage and Rice 157

Salmon Fried Rice 158

Chicken Cheesy Rice 159

Orange Ginger Rice 160

Coconut Rice 161

Mexican Rice 162

- **OTHER GRAINS AND CARBS** 163

Herbed Israeli Couscous with Apples and Cranberries 163

Curried Broccoli Couscous 164

Moroccan Couscous 166

Couscous with Salmon, Tomatoes, and Zucchini 167

Steph'z Southwestern "Couz-Couz" 168

Polenta Pizza 169

Fried Polenta Cakes with Beans and Salsa 170

Stuffing with Chicken and Cranberries 171

Stuffing and Sausage 172

Cheesy Broccoli, Sausage, and Quinoa 173

Quinoa with Pistachios and Dried Cherries 174

Almond Sesame Quinoa 176

Cheesy Quinoa with Sweet Potato, Black Beans, and Corn 177

Curried Quinoa with Chicken 178

"Caretaker's Dream" Stir-Fry 179

Homemade Falafel 180

Baked Potatoes 181

- **CURRIES, STEWS, AND SOUPS** 182

Chicken and Veggie Curry 182

Thai Coconut Curry 184

Chicken Tikka Masala 185

Quick Chicken and Rice Stew 186

Indonesian Sweet Potato and Cabbage Stew 186

Chili con Carne 188

One-Pot Deconstructed Enchilada 189

Tortilla Soup 190

Broccoli and Cheddar Soup 191

Cuban Black Bean Soup 192

Lentil Soup 193

- **MORE MEAT AND FISH** 194

Creamed Chipped Beef 194

Lemon Butter Trout 195

Garlic and Thyme Fish on a Stick 196

Trout Piccata 198

Hobo Dinner 199

Unstuffed Peppers with Beef 200

Frozen Steaks Alfresco 201

7 • DESSERTS AND SWEET DRINKS   203

- **DESSERTS**   204
  Scotch-a-Roos   204
  Trail Mix Cookies   205
  Peanut Butter Squares   206
  Oatmeal Chocolate Peanut Butter Cookies   207
  No-Bake Cookies   209
  Caramel Corn   210
  Sopapillas   211
  Pineapple Upside-Down Cake   212
  Chocolate Raspberry Delight   214
- **COCOA VARIATIONS**   215
  Classic Cocoa   215
  Mexican Cocoa   216
  Salted Caramel Cocoa   217
  Winter Butter Cocoa   217

Appendix A: Backcountry Ratio Guide   219
Appendix B: Drinking Water Treatment Methods   221
Index   224
Notes   228

·············· ACKNOWLEDGMENTS

Special thanks to our many friends and family who inspired and taught us how to spend time in the outdoors. Thanks to Ethan's mom, Anne Bjornson, who would take him camping from a young age and always wake up the family with the smell of bacon cooking in a blue enamel pan on our Coleman stove. It was the best way to wake up while camping, period. And thanks to Sarah's pop, Gunnar Baldwin, and mom, Heather Baldwin, and Walter Hipple, Ethan's dad. Thanks to the St. Clairs, the Tillman-Leddys, the Albers, the McMeekins, the Reads, the Ellises, the Bjornson-Pennells, the Dahlingers, Scott Ellis, Raven Naramore, Erik Weil, Josh Fishkin, Tall Paul, Gardner Waldeier, Sarah Keener, Hannah Quimby, Zak Klein, and Ethan's Student Conservation Association (SCA) crew leaders, Don Hunger and Ginny Broadhurst. Special thanks to our editor, Victoria Sandbrook Flynn, for her amazing attention to detail and enthusiasm for this book.

Many AMC staff, hut croo, shelter caretakers, and trail crew contributed recipes and ideas for this book—thank you.

And to the 65 kids we led over the years while on SCA Trail Crews: Thanks for the laughs, the memories, and the years of great friendships formed over a pot of Gado Gado pasta (a.k.a. "God, Oh God, It's Awful Pasta").

INTRODUCTION

It's a cold fall morning. Frost has settled over the small island in the middle of a North Country lake where your tent is pitched. As you lay in your warm sleeping bag, the smell of coffee on the stove fills your lungs, followed by—is that caramel? Cinnamon? Golden-brown, buttery sugar melting into a flaky roll?

Yes, 6 miles from the nearest road, sticky buns are baking in a reflector oven next to the fire. It doesn't matter what the weather brings today or how far down the lake you get: Life is good.

We wrote this book because we believe that eating well while on outdoor adventures keeps you safer; makes you happy; and leads to amazing, lifelong memories. Sure, you can add hot water to a bland, off-the-shelf, dehydrated meal from a local outdoor retailer, but we believe there is a better way.

There are plenty of outdoor cookbooks out there. We wrote this book to capture something new. Building on our history with the Appalachian Mountain Club and its long-standing tradition of backcountry hospitality, we hope to offer up recipes and a backcountry-cooking mindset that emphasizes the following:

- **Whole foods.** Simply *real food.* We've worked hard to minimize the pre-packaged and branded items included here. We'll leave it up to you to prioritize whether you choose to go organic or not, but you will be making most of what you eat from scratch, and it's worth it.

- **Preplanned menus.** This is not a bulk-food or ration system. Unlike other "open pantry" methods that have you throw a bunch of ingredients in your sack before winging it in the backcountry, our method involves careful planning for trips of three to five days, with each menu itemized and packed accordingly.

- **Deliciousness.** We'll get into this later, but the bottom line is you won't eat or enjoy food unless it is delicious, so we focus on flavors and freshness. Life is too short to shovel in a pile of pasta and hit the hay. (We know how much of a motivator food can be for kids on overnight trips, so we kept our experiences as parents top in our minds when choosing these recipes, as well.)

- **Nutrition.** These recipes are not necessarily low calorie or low fat, because you need calories and fat to battle strong headwinds on a backcountry paddle. Instead of just making you full, these fueling foods will make you *happy.*

ABOUT US

High up above treeline in the White Mountains, the Appalachian Mountain Club runs a system of remote backcountry huts where hikers find shelter, homemade food, and overnight accommodations, all miles from the nearest road. We, Sarah and Ethan, met while we were hut "croo" in AMC's hut system, and we spent six seasons there, cooking up delicious, wholesome meals for large groups hungry from a day of traversing the White Mountain ridges. We learned that homemade bread and a hot bowl of soup can bring a smile

to just about anyone's face, and that home-cooked lasagna, beef stroganoff, and turkey dinners taste about ten times better in the backcountry.

After our tenure in the huts, we worked our way across the country, leading backcountry trail crews for the Student Conservation Association (SCA). Living for a month or more as far as 12 miles into the backcountry in New Mexico, Indiana, Massachusetts, Utah, North and South Dakota, and Washington, facing dreary stretches of rainy weather with miles of trail to build, food became the high point of each day. Even though the temperatures were low and the rains kept coming, we learned the right hot meal could brighten the spirit, keeping people happy and motivated.

We've taken dozens of backpacking, climbing, kayak, and long-distance bike-camping trips with family and friends, both for outdoor leadership trainings and as leaders of Wilderness Orientation trips. We've cooked up sizzling, garlic-stuffed steaks on remote stretches of the Colorado River in the Grand Canyon and no-bake cookies on the beach in Point Reyes, California. On

TOP: Co-author Sarah's sticky buns keep her family motivated in the backcountry. Photo: Ethan Hipple
BOTTOM: Co-author Ethan has practiced fire safety with his kids from a young age. Photo: Sarah Hipple

the high ridges of New Hampshire's Evans Notch, we've whipped up light and delicious real-buttermilk pancakes with fresh-picked blueberries, and we've feasted on chicken bacon mac and cheese as we biked and camped up the coast of North Carolina's Cape Hatteras National Seashore.

On each of these trips, no matter who was with us, we found that backcountry food is not just a necessity but a focus. It keeps us going and it makes us happy. And we still remember what we ate on each trip, because we took the time to make it good. We hope this book inspires you to do the same.

Sarah is now a personal chef and caterer, cooking for private clients, country-chic weddings, political candidates, and wilderness-leader trainings. Ethan continues his work in the outdoors as a parks director and outdoor writer. He is co-author of AMC's *Outdoors with Kids Maine, New Hampshire, and Vermont* and a regular contributor to both AMC's Great Kids Great Outdoors blog and *AMC Outdoors* magazine columns. As our kids, Jackson and Tasha, have gotten older, we've handed them the spatula, and now they help us cook up tasty backcountry treats on every trip.

We hope you love these recipes as much as we do and that the tasty food you make will not only keep you going on the trail but will become a highlight of your trips and a lasting, lifelong memory.

·········· HOW TO USE THIS BOOK

We have organized this book to make it quick and easy to find recipes that work for any type of trip and for any diet. If you're just flipping through, icons will help you find the following categories of recipes:

V	Vegetarian	🕐	First Night Out (perishable recipes)
V+	Vegan	🏠	Make at Home
DF	Dairy Free	🌲	Make in the Field
GF	Gluten Free	🪶	Lightweight (dry ingredients weigh less than 0.5 lbs.)
NF	Nut Free	🏋	Heavyweight (dry ingredients weigh more than 2.0 lbs.)

While the metric system sure makes a lot of sense, it is not yet widely adopted here in the United States, so all measurements are in imperial system units. All recipes also have been weighed for you, so you can more easily calculate your food load on each trip.

Our goal is to help you find a recipe for any situation. The table of contents is a great way to browse by meal category: breakfast or dessert, make at home or make on the trail. The index is where you can find any recipe in any category that uses a specific ingredient or flavor. For example, if you look in the index for "beef," you'll find Honey Barbecue Beef Jerky under "Cold Lunches and Snacks on the Go" and Beef Stroganoff under "Hot Dinners at Camp."

The first three chapters of this book walk you through backcountry meal planning in a detailed manner, considering nutrition, flavor, pack weight, gear, and safety. Even if you've been cooking out of a pack or a canoe for a while, you might read through these sections to see if any of the wisdom we've gleaned from our years in the backcountry can help you make your trips easier and more delicious.

Whether you pick the simplest-to-prepare meals, the wow-factor dishes, or just the recipes that make your mouth water, we hope delicious food in the backcountry will always be a big part of what makes your trips unforgettable.

SECTION 1
FOOD IN THE
BACKCOUNTRY

Some people simply eat to live, while others live to eat. We are firmly in the "live to eat" category and have spent much of our lives making good food for our families, friends, and clients. Cooking and eating is a focus of every day, and we spend much of our spare time cooking. When we go on outdoor adventures, cooking is a big part of the experience. Rather than just shoveling in the calories required to get to the next trail junction, we like to take the time to eat well in the backcountry.

Why eat a peanut butter sandwich for dinner when you can have Gado Gado noodles in a delicious peanut sauce, with hints of garlic and ginger (see page 132)? Why cook Day-Glo orange mac and cheese from a box when it's just as easy to make the real thing: chewy, hearty noodles coated in a sharp cheddar sauce (see page 152)? Why have another morning of bland oatmeal when you can eat gooey and buttery caramel rolls, fresh-baked next to the fire (see page 80)?

Cooking in the backcountry is also a great way to spend time and bond with your kids. Our children have grown up helping with meal preparation on backpacking, paddling, or long-distance bike-camping trips. They help cut the onions, shred the cheese, knead the dough—and they share in the satisfaction of preparing delicious meals, miles from home. It's a confidence builder and a good lifelong skill.

NUTRITION

The human body is close to being a perpetual-motion machine. You put food and water into it, you get energy out. It just keeps going. With the right foods, a lot of water, and plenty of rest, it will take you many amazing places: high mountain peaks, hidden backcountry swimming holes, and deep forests carpeted with moss. With the planning resources in this book, your calorie needs will be covered, your food weight will be moderated, and you will have plenty of options for feeding anyone in your group who follows a special diet. Most importantly, those lightweight meals will be simple, easy to prepare, and delicious.

You may have to shift how you think about calories, sugar, carbohydrates, and fats when you plan your next backcountry adventure. While each year's fad diet tells us these things are bad and should be avoided, the recipes in this book focus on their value to us, as backcountry travelers. Of course, everything needs to be moderated, but an understanding of what makes your food fuel will help you plan backcountry meals to your best advantage.

Daily Calorie Needs

Calories—whether they are derived from proteins, fats, or carbohydrates—are absolute necessities for anyone taking part in high-energy activities, such as backpacking, climbing, and paddling. Instead of avoiding calories, we've designed our recipes and meal plans with the goal of making sure each meal has *enough* calories to keep you going toward your destination.

A calorie is simply a unit of energy contained in a set amount of food. Calorie needs vary greatly depending on your activity. Most adults in a moderately sedentary lifestyle need 1,600 to 2,400 calories per day to maintain a healthy weight. Adults on backcountry adventures typically need 3,200 to 6,000 calories per day to maintain vital levels of energy and warmth. Your biggest issue on a backcountry trip is how to get enough calories in your body.

DAILY CALORIE NEEDS			
Sedentary Activities (office work, housework)	Moderate Activities (walking, mowing, kayaking)	Active (running, biking, hiking)	Strenuous (backpacking, mountaineering, climbing)
Adult Male 2,000–2,400	2,200–2,800	2,400–3,000	4,000–6,000
Adult Female 1,600–2,000	1,800–2,200	2,000–2,400	3,500–5,500

Sources: U.S. Department of Health and Human Services and U.S. Department of Agriculture, 2015–2020 Dietary Guidelines for Americans, 8th ed. (2015). Appalachian Mountain Club Boston Chapter, An Introduction to Winter Hiking: Course Manual for the Winter Hiking and Backpacking Program (Boston: Appalachian Mountain Club, 2014).

Carbohydrates

Instead of banning carbs to the compost pile, we include many kinds of carbohydrates in our recipes because they provide the long-lasting energy required on long trips. There's a reason marathon runners eat heaping plates of spaghetti the night before a big race.

Starches are long-lasting sources of energy for your adventures. Foods that fall into this category include potatoes, whole grains, rice, and beans. The

Beans are a good source of backcountry fiber. Photo: James Saunders, Creative Commons on Flickr

majority of the recipes in this book rely on starches, as they are lightweight, healthy, and provide the energy you need to get where you're going.

Grains are the primary building block of most diets: Think bread, pasta, and cereal. The typical Western, frontcountry diet is full of processed grains (e.g., white bread, pasta, and all-purpose flour), which are stripped of many of their beneficial properties. Whole-grain foods pack a much bigger punch, no matter where you eat them. The closer the grain is to its natural state, the slower your body processes the starch, which gives you long-lasting, steady energy. Whole grains also provide more fiber and protein than their processed counterparts. In the backcountry, whole grains can make all the difference.

Sugar is universally loved, but its value is temporary. The quick burst of energy you get from sugar is not nearly as useful as the punch you get from a bowl of oatmeal or a dinner of pasta and cheese. Use sugar as a morale booster and as a treat, not as your primary source of energy. The one exception may be the perfect backcountry snack: the Snickers bar. We know, we know. It's not the first thing that comes to mind when you think "wholesome," but in dire situations, one bar pairs 8 grams of protein (from the peanuts) with chocolate, which naturally makes people happy. If you can't quite stomach a Snickers, this book includes plenty of similarly nutritious partnerships that make what you're eating (and carrying) more valuable than a sugary treat on its own.

Fiber has no caloric value, but we all need 20 to 30 grams of this stuff every day to stay healthy, feel full, and to keep bowel movements regular. Think of it as roughage that scrubs the walls of your digestive system. You don't want to get blocked up while in the backcountry; this can lead to serious health problems and having to cut a trip short. Cooking foods with adequate fiber—including whole grains, fruits, and vegetables—will keep you feeling comfortable.

Proteins

Proteins don't give you energy, necessarily, but they are the building blocks for restoring and building body tissue and muscle. We should all eat plenty of protein, on and off the trail. Fresh meat and tofu are limited in the backcountry diet due to weight and lack of refrigeration, but legumes, quinoa, jerky, canned meats, and cured meats, such as salami and pepperoni, can be delicious substitutes.

Think of any fresh-caught trout as a bonus source of protein. Photo: Ethan Hipple

Complete proteins contain adequate amounts of each of the nine amino acids necessary for your body to function. In the frontcountry, we usually get complete proteins from eggs, dairy, meat, or vegetable products, such as soy-based tofu, but these ingredients don't all travel well in the backcountry without refrigeration. Dehydrated, canned, and cured meats—from jerky to canned chicken, to salami—are all delicious substitutes. Dehydrated egg and dairy products are also much longer-lived in the backcountry. Quinoa is one of the only vegetable-based foods that is also a complete protein, and for that reason, many recipes in this book include it.

Incomplete proteins have some but not all of the essential amino acids you need. Nuts, beans, and other legumes, such as lentils, are all incomplete proteins. Pairing certain starches and carbohydrates also can give you a complete protein for your meal. Popular examples are rice and beans, hummus and pita, and nuts and grain (also known as the peanut butter sandwich).

Vegetables and Fruits

Always include plant-based foods in your backcountry menus, even though they can be a bit heavier and harder to carry. A food dehydrator will make quick work of reducing the weight of your fruits and vegetables, turning them into vital backcountry staples that will keep indefinitely. Full of vitamins, minerals, and fiber, vegetables and fruits should be basic building blocks of all of your menus.

Unless you are going out for a very short trip (one to two nights), we highly recommend dehydrating your vegetables. Onions, peppers, and celery

Build complete proteins by pairing sweet potatoes and beans. Photo: Jennifer Wehunt

are our go-to standards for just about any recipe, but you can dry almost anything: kale, eggplant, even tomato sauce!

As for fruit, dried apple chips, mango jerky, and made-at-home fruit leather are great go-to trail snacks. Fruit will give you fiber and carbs, as well as a quick burst of sugar-fueled energy to get you up that last pitch of steep trail.

Dairy

Our personal favorite food group, dairy is a mixed bag in terms of value in the backcountry. While it packs a lot of calcium and protein (especially in items such as cheese), it doesn't keep well and can be heavy. Despite the weight, we always bring a *lot* of sharp cheddar cheese because it's full of great flavor, has a lot of protein, and just makes us happy. In most weather, a block of sharp cheddar will keep for up to five days without refrigeration. Softer cheeses, such as Muenster, will last two to three days in a pack. We'd rather carry the extra weight of cheese than face the bleak, meaningless existence without it.

We always prefer real butter to highly processed margarines with lots of preservatives because you know what's in it—cream—and it tastes like heaven. For trips longer than three days, however, you may want to bring freeze-dried butter powder, as it is lighter, will keep indefinitely, and won't melt all over your pack. Read more about butter powder, powdered milk, and powdered cheeses under "Dehydrated Foods," beginning on page 16. And if dairy is not for you, hop over to "Special Diets: Dairy Free" on page 8, for a few suggestions regarding backcountry-friendly substitutes.

Fats

Fats are your body's slow-burning energy source. They are more useful to your body when you're trying to stay warm in a tent at night than when you are traversing a massive ridge. You will be burning so many calories while traveling in the backcountry, you don't have to watch fat intake as much as you might at home. A general rule of thumb in the backcountry is to eat enough fat to make your food taste good, and you'll be just fine.

So, use your preferred cooking medium liberally, whether it's butter or olive oil. Spread your peanut butter a little thick—and don't worry.

FLAVOR

We always consider the calories, quantities, food weight, and preservability of food in the backcountry, but a food's most important characteristic might be what we call "deliciousness." You may not use that word often, but it may be the most important factor in staying energized and healthy while on back-country adventures. If the food isn't delicious, you're not going to want to eat it.

There is some science behind the deliciousness factor, as well. Humans naturally crave what we need to survive. As most of us will recognize, we gravitate toward salty and sweet foods. We do this because the flavors sub-liminally signal something to us: that these foods pack a lot of calories. It's not a coincidence we crave the sweet-salty punch of gorp on the trail. Our bodies tell us that, because this food tastes sweet and salty, it must have valuable nutrients (calories, fat, and carbs). Therefore, we must eat more of it. Since

For flavorful dishes, don't forget to pack the pepper! Photo: Jennifer Wehunt

we depend on calories to survive, this signal is an important survival instinct built into our physiology.

Most people learn about four basic flavors: sweet, salty, sour, and bitter. But an important fifth flavor, umami, has been increasingly recognized in recent years. Umami is often described as a meaty or brothy flavor, the richness of a beef broth or the fullness of Parmesan. It's the flavor that turns simple hot salt water into *a soup.* The flavor was given its Japanese name in the early 1900s, but umami transcends regional cuisines and has been increasingly identified and used in foods around the world. Umami is everywhere but is particularly noticeable in items such as soy sauce, marmite, and vegemite. It is also found in Parmesan, cured meats, cooked tomatoes, mushrooms, and interestingly, breast milk.

Armed with these facts, you can tell your body that what you are eating is good and that you should have more by balancing these key elements in your food. For this reason, we use plenty of umami-creating ingredients in this book: lots of broths, cheeses, and plenty of soy sauce in recipes and as a condiment. And after a long day in the backcountry your body will be even more appreciative of these flavors as you relax and refuel.

SPECIAL DIETS

Many recipes in this book contain known allergens or are not designed to accommodate specific dietary restrictions. Read the ingredient lists carefully; icons for recipes compatible with special diets will help you find meal ideas that are safe for your needs. Most of the remaining recipes can be adapted as easily as any recipe you make at home.

Eating healthy gives you the energy you need on the trail. Photo: Ferrous Büller, Creative Commons on Flickr

V V+ Vegetarian and Vegan

Vegetarians and vegans will find plenty of recipes in this book. In fact, because meat doesn't keep well in the backcountry, many of the recipes are already vegetarian. If meat is listed in a recipe, simply keep it out or replace it with your preferred vegetarian protein: tofu, textured vegetable protein, tempeh, etc.

DF Dairy Free

If you are vegan, lactose intolerant, or have a milk allergy, you're likely already familiar with adaptations for recipes requiring at least one dairy product. Most of the recipes included in this book are naturally dairy free, but some do call for butter, cheese, milk, or other dairy products. Reliable substitutes for fresh dairy products are easy to find at most grocery stores, but powdered substitutes for backcountry assembly can be harder to locate. Powdered coconut and almond milks are available at some specialty grocers and through online suppliers.

GF Gluten Free

Many recipes in this book are naturally gluten free, and these are marked with a "Gluten Free" icon. For recipes that include wheat or products with gluten, you can substitute different products that work for your diet, just as you would at home. For wheat-pasta substitutions, we recommend quinoa pasta, which is exceptionally high in protein and carbs.

Paleo, Atkins, Cleansing, and Other Weight-Loss Diets

We do not recommend following a strict weight-loss diet of any kind while you are on a backcountry adventure. Backpacking, climbing, and other strenuous activities require a very high number of calories, and restrictions on calorie intake for most weight-loss diets can prove harmful or even dangerous in a backcountry situation. Withholding certain food groups without consciously replacing the nutrients elsewhere can be a big a strain on your body.

Eat a wholesome, well-balanced, carb- and protein-rich diet while on your trip, and resume your weight-loss diet when you return to a more sedentary pace back home.

SECTION 2
PLANNING YOUR TRIP

MEAL-PLANNING GRID

Welcome to the nitty-gritty of eating well in the backcountry. Let's say you are heading out on a five-day trip, and you need to start planning your menu and shopping. Instead of making two separate lists, use this grid system that serves both as your menu and your shopping list.

Starting your grid is simple. Create rows for meals and columns for days. Using the recipes in this book, fill in the grid's fields, listing all of the ingredients for each dish you'll serve. Go through your pantry at home and highlight any grid ingredients you're missing then bring the grid with you when you shop. Also be sure to pack a copy of the grid so that, once you're in the backcountry, you know which meal is which and what all those bags of ingredients are for.

For trips longer than five days, consider repeating daily menus, as this makes planning and shopping easier. But this is totally up to personal taste. You can always plan something different for every day, if you prefer.

Many backcountry cookbooks call for an open-pantry style of meal planning, which is great for trips ten days and longer. Basically, you use a formula to figure out a certain weight of ingredients per person, per day. Then, once you're out in the field, you improvise your menu using the ingredients at hand. While this is a good system for monthlong backcountry expeditions, it does not work well for the three- to five-day trips most of us take: There would simply be too much to carry for such a short duration. Instead, plan your meals ahead of time using a grid, prepare some ingredients and mixes at home, and make the rest on the trail, according to your meal plan.

Photo: Sara Thompson,
Creative Commons on Flickr

MEAL-PLANNING GRID					
	Wednesday	Thursday	Friday	Saturday	Sunday
Breakfast	At home	Fried bagels Cream cheese Sliced tomatoes Fresh-picked blueberries	Granola and powdered milk Fresh-picked blueberries	Hash brown scramble Dehydrated hash browns, eggs, onion, cheese	Cranberry-orange skillet muffins Make-at-home muffin mix, butter
Lunch	Bagel sandwiches Salami cheese, cucumber Chocolate peanut butter granola bars	Teriyaki beef jerky Black bean spread Carrots	Pita bread and hummus Cucumbers, avocado	Crackers Slivered garlic Salami and cheese	On the road: pizza!
Dinner	Chicken black bean quesadillas Bean, chicken, cheese tortillas	Israeli couscous with apples, cranberries, walnuts, herbs	Tortilla soup Corn tortillas Chicken	Chicken bacon mac and cheese	At home
Dessert	Hot cocoa, tea Chocolate bars	Hot cocoa, tea Scotch-a-Roos	Hot cocoa, tea No-bake cookies	Hot cocoa, tea Sopapillas	At home

YOUR BACKCOUNTRY PANTRY

At home, you can turn to your pantry—or run to the store—whenever you're in a pinch. But when heading into the backcountry, you have to anticipate and pack everything you might want—or you'll have to wait for it until you're back in the frontcountry. Planning your meals ahead of time can include having the right cooking mediums for several meals, saving space and time by using the same mix more than once, and even repurposing leftovers. As you're picking recipes for the trail, the following considerations will help keep your food weight low and your prep work simple.

Choosing Ingredients for the Backcountry

If the goal is to stick with whole and healthy foods for your trip, you have some options. Time, weight, and cost will all play a factor in which ingredients you choose, but so will freshness, durability, and availability.

While this book focuses on using everyday ingredients, some of the recipes in the dinner section call for items that may be difficult to find in your local grocery store, particularly in smaller stores or rural areas. But don't worry! There are usually tasty substitutions, although fresh ingredients will always be heavier. With a little planning, you can usually find just about any shelf-stable ingredient from a reputable online retailer. (See "Dehydrated Foods," page 16, for suggestions and substitutions.)

Common sauces, such as alfredo, present another chance to balance your time investment, weight, and backcountry convenience (see "Hot Dinners at Camp"). We've provided recipes for make-at-home powdered sauces that incorporate easily into meals; just bring your mix on the trail and follow the directions for the perfect dish. You could also make your favorite version of the sauce at home and dehydrate it into sauce leather. We don't cover this preparation because it's time-intensive for a three- to five-day outing, but for a longer trip, it's worth the effort. Ready-made, powdered sauces from the grocery store can work as fast, cheap stand-ins for the mixes we've included in this book (just substitute the premade version for our homemade mixes), but there are trade-offs: Nutritional values vary between brands and varieties, and purchased mixes likely won't be made with the whole foods we prioritize in this book.

Sometimes the ingredients matter greatly, and improvising won't serve you well. For example, substituting instant rice or oatmeal when the recipe doesn't call for them will usually result in an overcooked bowl of mush. Polenta, on the other hand, takes a great deal of time and fuel to cook in the backcountry, so we highly suggest using premade polenta, available in most grocery stores. Throughout the book, we indicate where using quicker options is appropriate.

The backcountry can be hard on many of your favorite foods, and some experience with how long things keep in a pack can help you avoid disappointing (or even dangerous) discoveries midtrip. Fresh bagels, for instance, can go bad after a day or two. Store-bought packaged bagels keep for a week, but they've got more preservatives. Better to bring fresh bagels and eat them in the first day or two of your trip.

Consider, too, the durability of the food you're bringing. Pita and pretzel chips are sturdier than your average cracker. Thin, stone-ground wheat crackers are sturdier than sesame crackers. Ritz and saltine crackers don't hold up well. Pita bread is easier to pack flat than a loaf of whole-wheat sandwich bread. But if you can't live without something specific, there's usually a way to bring it along.

While most folks likely won't be out in the backcountry for an extended period of time, keep in mind that "healthy" goes beyond "sufficient caloric intake." The cheapest, lightest gear can pose health hazards over extended use (e.g., nonstick and aluminum pans, plastic containers that are not BPA-free). Certain foods can also pose health concerns if eaten too frequently, though alternatives are usually available. So if you want to eat tuna for five straight days, visit seafoodwatch.org to identify the varieties that are caught sustainably and lowest in mercury. The wisdom you follow at home in these matters usually applies in the backcountry, as well.

Finally, many of these recipes could be significantly dressed up, depending on your tastes, the other ingredients you have on hand, and how much you want to carry. Pancakes, omelets and scrambles, oatmeal, burritos and tacos, pastas, and even hot cocoa are just a few of the backcountry dishes that afford plenty of leeway for adding your favorite flavors. There's no practical way to provide you with the nutrition benefits and weights of every possible option; we mean it when we say the varieties are endless! In some cases, as with oatmeal, we've provided baseline recipes to which you can add as much or as little variety as you'd like. Nutrition data and weights for these variations should be easy enough for you to gather when you purchase the ingredients. In other cases, as with the scrambles, we've suggested combinations that are particularly flavorful and/or that capitalize on backcountry staples, such as dehydrated vegetables, so you can make the most of what you're carrying. In these latter examples, nutrition stats are provided for the combinations shown.

Repackaging

Repackage all of your food to save room and weight in your pack. Food from the grocery store comes in an amazing array of heavy, bulky packaging with excessive airspace, and you won't want to carry all of that around with you on your trip. Minimizing the trash you bring into the backcountry will minimize the trash you have to bring out. That said, bags can serve as a great way to organize ingredients for specific recipes. Invest in high-quality, zippered freezer storage bags, which can be washed and reused many times, and repackage your ingredients into them before your trip. Many recipes in this book have specific suggestions on repackaging for easiest backcountry assembly.

As you're preparing ingredients for the trail, consider which can be packaged together in a single bag to keep measuring, mixing, and pouring outdoors to a minimum. Dry ingredients added all at once are usually the easiest place to start. We've called out many of these as spice and sauce mixes in

Storing all ingredients for a given meal together will help keep you organized. Photo: OakleyOriginals, Creative Commons on Flickr

recipes. Some liquids—such as coconut, vegetable, or sesame oil—can be repacked in small, airtight containers before you leave home. In some cases, it makes more sense to carry one larger bag of an ingredient—say, butter powder—that you will use for multiple meals. The exact arrangements are up to you, but generally plan to pack fresh ingredients and liquids separately from dry ingredients. If a recipe's preparation benefits greatly from a specific repackaging method, we offer instruction in the text.

When you repackage dry mixes—spice blends or liquid-ready batter, for example—label the bag with a permanent marker. Put a copy of the ingredients and the recipe into the bag. This way, if a recipe requires several bags (one for pasta, one for spices, one for cooking mediums), you know which bags to look for and how to use their contents without taking this book along. When you repackage pasta, note the required cook time on your zippered storage back or recipe notes; you'll need it later!

When pouring a dry mix out of a zippered storage bag, roll the mouth of the bag under so no powder gets caught in the bag's locking mechanism. This will keep your bags closed tightly and save you a backpack covered in iced tea or hot chocolate mix!

If you've mixed and stored wet ingredients in a zippered bag—a dough or batter, for instance—don't unzip the bag to pour out the mix. To empty the entirety of the mix into a pan, cut a corner and squeeze the contents out. To get everything out, roll the bag like a tube of toothpaste. For pancakes or cookies, put the bag in a bowl big enough to hold it, roll the top down, and use a spoon, cup, or ladle to measure out correct portions.

All-Purpose Mixes

Many of the recipes in this book rely on mixes you prepare ahead of time at home and bring along with you into the field. This not only saves time outdoors but reduces packaging and weight. If you plan ahead, you can bring enough baking mix to make muffins, quick breads, and cakes. Or pack a cornmeal mix and stretch it to make both pancakes and cornbread. One bag of dry marinara sauce can last for several dishes during your trip. You might have to do some fast math at home to make sure you have enough for all the meals you plan to cook, but you'll pack in fewer bags and have just what you need, when you need it.

Dehydrated Foods

Packing dehydrated food will reduce the weight you have to carry and will let you enjoy meats and vegetables long after the first night of a trip. Consider choosing some or all of the following dehydrated foods:

- **Vegetables** of all sorts are available dried in bulk. Dehydrated potatoes, for example, can be mashed, hashed, or made into pancakes, and also work as a soup and stew thickener. Dried peas, carrots, peppers, onions, tomatoes, broccoli, mushrooms, celery, onions, and garlic will all be staples in your backcountry diet. Stock up.

- **Dried meats** go far beyond jerky, with a wide variety available online. From ground beef to stew meat to ground chicken and turkey, these freeze-dried meats are lightweight, relatively cheap, and boost the protein content of your backcountry meals. Look for versions that are antibiotic free; free-range (poultry), grass-fed (beef), pasture-raised (pork); with no added ingredients.

- **Dried fruit** is available almost anywhere and is a backcountry staple you can't do without.

- **Orange and lemon juice powders** are simply dehydrated juice. These are available from online retailers that sell freeze-dried and dehydrated foods. Look for versions labeled 100 percent fruit or juice.

- **Beans** are the workhorse of your backcountry menu. From refried to lentils, garbanzos, and pintos, beans are healthy, cheap, and make a complete protein when eaten with rice. Eat refried beans with rice, in quesadillas, and as a soup thickener. Dehydrated beans can also be used in soups, stews, and sautés.

- **Egg crystals** are preferable to other powdered egg substitutes. Whole, fresh eggs take on a crystalline structure when you dry them slowly at low heat, as in a dehydrator. When rehydrated they taste great, with a nice texture. Plus, egg crystals are 100 percent egg, while some powders are thickened with starches and fillers. It may take a little more work to find or dehydrate these real eggs, but you won't regret it.

- **Cheddar cheese powder** has changed how we cook in the backcountry. If you're thinking old-school "shaker cheese," hold it right there. Trustworthy powdered cheeses include only cheese, buttermilk, salt, disodium phosphate (an anticaking agent), and maybe whey as a last ingredient. As always, read labels closely and choose varieties that are 100 percent cheese or thereabouts instead of those overly reliant on whey powder. Or make your own! For years, Parmesan was our go-to cheese powder. But after trying cheddar powder, available in many grocery stores, we're converts. This stuff is great as an all-purpose condiment. Sprinkle it on anything from pasta to soups to potatoes and couscous. Varieties include New England's own King Arthur Flour and Cabot.

- **Butter powder** can be used in sauces, in baking—even as a sprinkled condiment, similar to salt and pepper. It's a boon in the backcountry, as it is

When purchasing a dehydrator, look for a model with several trays and a fan. Photo: Sarah Hipple

lighter, will keep indefinitely, and won't melt all over your pack like regular butter. It also tastes great. Butter powder is certainly more processed than its fresh counterpart, but high-quality varieties include only real butter, nonfat milk solids, sodium caseinate (a milk protein), and disodium phosphate (an anticaking additive). Stay away from products listing additional preservatives and additives. You cannot make it at home, however, as it requires a more advanced process than a home dehydrator can tackle.

- **Powdered milk** is available pretty much everywhere, but if you want powdered whole milk, you have to go online or make it yourself. Be aware: The milk-drying process oxidizes cholesterol, which makes it a less than ideal ingredient for regular use in frontcountry cooking. If you are concerned about oxidized cholesterol in the backcountry, pick powdered nonfat milk, as its fresh counterpart has less cholesterol to begin with. You can find powdered nonfat milk in most grocery stores.

- **Dried sour cream** is a great for sauces and dishes such as beef stroganoff (see page 147).

You can purchase prepackaged dried foods or you can invest the time (and maybe less money) if you dehydrate food on your own. This book includes a few recipes for dehydrated backcountry snacks, but reliable sources for dehydrating almost any food exist in print and online.

There are many dehydrators on the market, ranging from the price of a takeout pizza to hundreds of dollars. We have found through experience that a cheap dehydrator with a fan works well. The "with a fan" clause is important: Dehydrators without a fan take much longer to dry food and are not recommended.

For quantities described in this book, a small or medium dehydrator should be fine. Aim for a model with three to five shelves. If you are planning longer trips and need a larger quantity of dehydrated foods, a bigger model (nine to ten trays) will make the process go quicker. The more trays you have, the more food you can prepare at once.

Most at-home dehydrators work on the same principle: With a combination of low heat and moving air, they simply suck the water out of any food. You don't want to bake the food—just to dry it out, reducing the water content. Properly dehydrated foods can last a year or more.

Freeze-drying is another method of dehydrating foods, but the equipment is generally more expensive and not practical for home dehydrating.

Some of our favorite essentials prepared at home with a dehydrator include:

- **Vegetable mixes.** Slice or dice, then dehydrate the ingredients you need for soups, stews, or sautés, Our favorite mix is onion, carrots, and celery.
- **Beef jerky.** Use steak or hamburger for a surprisingly easy and tasty treat. Our favorite version uses flank or skirt steak.
- **Fruit leather.** It's just delicious. You'll find a few of our favorites in "Cold Lunches and Snacks on the Go."

In addition to making your own dehydrated foods, you can buy bulk quantities of dehydrated foods for a very reasonable cost. Higher-end and specialty grocery stores carry a surprising variety of dehydrated foods, from coconut milk to high-quality egg crystals. If you don't have access to one of these stores, online retailers are a good bet, and many offer low-cost or free shipping. Many specialty online retailers focus solely on dehydrated bulk foods, and the proliferation of survivalist websites has been a boon to backpackers. Instead of driving hours to a specialty backpacking or health food store, you can now order a 5-pound can of dehydrated ground beef crumbles or mixed vegetables and have it delivered to your door.

To find other online retailers, simply search for "dehydrated foods," "preparedness food," "survival food," or "backpacking food" and you'll find a wealth of possibilities.

Customizing for Your Own Preferences

As discussed above, there are some trade-offs when it comes to backcountry cooking, including using some ingredients you might or might not turn to at home. We've included the following ingredients in this book because we feel comfortable using them when cooking for our own kids in the backcountry. But should you prefer to avoid them, you can often opt for substitutions, noted below, or simply choose other recipes. Likewise, we haven't explicitly recommended buying items that are 100 percent organic. That's a choice we believe is best left up to you.

- **Cornstarch**, also known as corn flour, is commonly used to thicken sauces (see our recipe for beef stroganoff on page 147). You can substitute rice flour or wheat flour in the recipes throughout this book, but cornstarch is our preferred thickener. Organic, GMO-free, and gluten-free options are available.

- **Corn syrup** doesn't necessarily mean "high-fructose corn syrup." Many people shy away from corn syrup due to the preponderance of genetically modified corn, as well as the negative health concerns surrounding high-fructose corn syrup (HFCS). But regular corn syrup is 100 percent glucose, whereas HFCS converts most of the glucose into fructose. Look

Choose bacon that is free of antibiotics, preservatives, nitrites, and nitrates. Photo: Travis, Creative Commons on Flickr

for all-natural, GMO-free brands that contain only corn syrup, salt, and vanilla or choose a substitute, such as cane syrup.

- **Precooked bacon** is a tasty addition to an endless number of backcountry dishes. It is shelf stable, meaning it doesn't need to be refrigerated—much like beef jerky. It has significantly less fat than uncooked bacon, as most of the fat has been cooked off, enabling the bacon to stay unrefrigerated without going rancid. This doesn't mean uncooked bacon doesn't have an expiration date, just that it lasts a lot longer. Same as you would when buying uncooked bacon, look for brands that are free of antibiotics, preservatives, nitrites, and nitrates.

Spice Kits

There are a couple of different ways to assemble a spice kit. You can pack exactly the spices and amounts you need for a trip based on your meal plan, or you can make or buy a nylon kit outfitted with plastic bags containing all of the usual suspects. If you go the latter route, simply make sure it's restocked and throw it in your pack. Here are our spice kit essentials:

- Salt and pepper
- Cinnamon
- Paprika
- Garlic powder or garlic salt
- Cumin
- Basil
- Oregano
- Curry
- White and brown sugar

Condiments

Condiments are key on a backcountry trip. They add spice or flavor to every meal, are lightweight, and allow people to customize a dish to their own tastes. Bring plenty. Here are some common options:

- **Soy sauce or liquid aminos** (an alternative to soy sauce also made from soybeans): After a long day on the trail, you'll need a good dose of salt.
- **Hot sauce:** Most vinegar-based versions do not require refrigeration.
- **Nutritional yeast:** This nutty, cheeselike powder is good sprinkled on pasta, rice, and potato dishes and is high in B vitamins.
- **Ketchup, mayonnaise, and mustard:** Choose single-use packets for easy packing.
- **Powdered cheese:** Our favorite, the powdered versions of Parmesan and cheddar will keep indefinitely in the backcountry and are full of umami flavor enhancers.

- **Chocolate hazelnut spread:** This is a great sweet condiment for dipping crackers, pretzels, and fruit; for spreading on pancakes, on fried bagels, and on pitas; or just for enjoying plain! Use store-bought brands or make your own (see page 100).

YOUR BACKCOUNTRY KITCHEN

When packing for your trip, you'll have a go-to list of supplies that will keep you safe and comfortable. Whether you're new to the backcountry or go camping every other weekend, you should always be prepared with food, water, shelter, navigation tools, and weather-appropriate clothing. If you're not familiar with the gear you'll need in the backcountry, or if you're looking for ways to pack smarter and lighter, AMC's *Mountain Skills Manual* (AMC Books, 2017) is great place to start.

That said, your kitchen gear can make a big difference in what you can cook, how you can cook it, how easily you can clean up afterward, and how you affect the area in which you cook.

Essential Backcountry Kitchen Gear

Every adult member of your trip should carry the following items:

- **Lighter:** As a rule of thumb, every adult should carry at least one lighter. A lighter is one of the 10 essentials for backcountry safety, and making sure everyone has his or her own means you won't have to constantly pass the group's sole lighter around or remember who had it last when it's time to light the stove. Cheap convenience-store lighters are better options than matches because they still work even if they are damp.
- **Mug:** A good mug is a must. Fill it with your preferred hot brew, broth, or food. Lightweight plastic mugs are preferable to heavy metal, but personal preference rules here. Before you leave, measure exactly how much liquid your cup holds so it can double as a measuring cup.
- **Pocketknife:** Although you will have a cutting knife (see the group list that follows), every adult should carry a good, sharp pocketknife. Having multiple folks help cut onions or peppers really speeds up meal prep time.
- **Spoon/fork:** A lightweight spoon is best and often all we'll bring. A fork is optional. Your spoon also will serve as a measuring spoon in the field. Be sure to measure what quantity it holds at home, before you leave on your trip.
- **Snacks:** Pack these in their own dry bags or stuff sacks lined with trash compactor bags so you have easy access to (dry!) snacks when you need them.

You might premeasure and pack spices by meal, as on the facing page, or in kits. Photo: Jennifer Wehunt

Your shared group gear should always include:

- **Cutting mat and sharp knife:** Choose a lightweight, rollable cutting mat and a sharp knife with a sheath.
- **Dishes:** Lightweight snap-lock, resealable food-storage containers make great backpacking dishes. Most grocery stores carry BPA-free varieties, and you can find silicone versions at outdoor stores. If you're going very lightweight, just bring a spoon and eat out of the pot.
- **Dishwashing kit:** Pick a biodegradable soap, in keeping with Leave No Trace ethics (see page 34), and repackage it in a smaller container that seals tightly. This doubles as hand soap, too, so bring plenty. We prefer a scrubby pad to a sponge because scrubbies dry faster and don't breed as much bacteria—or odors. Cut a 5-by-5-inch section of window screen to use as a strainer for dishwater and pack everything in a zippered storage bag.
- **Fuel:** The type of fuel you pack will depend on your stove, but fuel should always be stored below food in any pack, in case of spills. Before you leave, check all O-rings and seals on the fuel cans to make sure you have no active leaks.
- **Paracord** (also called P-cord): Bring 25 to 50 feet for bagging your food at night, stringing up a tarp, and more.

Your group's shared gear will include lightweight pots and pans. Photo: Jennifer Wehunt

- **Pliers:** These useful tools can serve as pot handles and a hot pad.
- **Pots and pans:** For up to four people we bring:
  - Lightweight, 10-inch, nonstick frying pan: Over years of trial and error, we've found that the best pans are cheap, lightweight pans from the hardware store. If it breaks, it can be replaced. Higher-end backpacking pans and stainless steel pans may be healthier than their counterparts coated with nonstick surfaces or made from aluminum, but they may be heavier and harder to scrub; be prepared to use extra butter or oil when frying.
  - Pair of lightweight, nesting saucepans with lids, preferably one 3-quart and one 4-quart: These saucepans will serve many uses: mixing bowls, heating hot water, and more.
- **Reflector oven:** Although Dutch ovens are too heavy for backpacking (more on them under "Paddling Extras," page 27), a reflector oven is light enough to pack. These are used next to a fire, so only plan on baked meals where fires are permitted along your route.
- **Serving spoon and spatula:** Bring one or two large wooden or metal serving spoons for cooking and serving, and a metal spatula for flipping food, such as pancakes or burgers.
- **Stove:** Buy and bring the right stove for you. You'll find a quick review of backcountry stoves below.
- **Tarp:** A high-quality, ripstop-nylon backpacking tarp will weigh a little extra in your pack, but there's nothing better than sipping a hot cup of cocoa under a well-pitched tarp in a rainstorm.
- **Trash compactor bags:** Use durable, waterproof, 2.5- to 3-millimeter-thick bags to protect food from fuel, clothes from food, and everything from getting wet! Buy as many as you'll need and bring a few spares along for good measure.
- **Water bag:** These are very handy items to have along: fill them up in a stream, hang them from a tree, and you have an instant water source and hand washing station combined. (See Appendix B on page 221 for instructions on water treatment.)
- **Zippered storage bags:** Bring plenty of quart- and gallon-sized zippered storage bags. One gallon-sized, resealable bag should be big enough to carry all of your individual trash for the week.

Stoves

There are many types of stoves on the market. The following overview will help you choose which works best for your needs, your trips, and your kitchen.

White gas stoves are highly recommended for the availability of fuel: Regular white gas can be found in most outdoor stores and big-box retailers. A plus: If something goes wrong, these stoves often are easily to repair in the field, as long as you carry the repair kit with you. They have a reputation of being very durable when kept clean over time. Most outfitters and outdoor schools use some version of a white gas stove, as they are hardy and reliable enough for institutional use.

Compressed fuel stoves are lightweight and typically run on propane or butane. The stoves themselves are typically affordable, but the fuel canisters are not refillable and can get quite expensive to replace—not to mention quite heavy. These stoves are convenient and easy to use, but weight and fuel expense has always kept us away.

Wood camp stoves on the market today are truly innovative. Using small kindling no bigger than your pinky, you fill the stove's internal compartment to build a surprisingly hot cooking flame, assisted by an integrated battery-operated fan.

TOP LEFT: A compressed fuel, or canister, stove runs on gas. Photo: Jennifer Wehunt

BOTTOM LEFT: A wood-burning camp stove doubles as a battery charger. Photo: Ethan Hipple

Some models will even convert the heat of the fire into a trickle of electricity to charge your camera, GPS unit, or phone. The primary drawback of these wood-powered stoves is that if you hit a stretch of rain and all available wood is waterlogged, you will have a heck of a time cooking dinner.

Alcohol stoves are cheap, easy to use, and very lightweight—perfect for the minimalist backcountry cook. They generally work better for solo or duo travelers, as most models are just too small to fit a large pan or pot. They offer limited flame adjustability and are best for boiling water for one-pot wonders. For a solo hiker on a lightweight trip with a simple menu, they're perfect.

Measuring Cups and Spoons

We intentionally left measuring cups and spoons off of our list. Portioning and packing ahead of time can alleviate the need to measure everything in the field. Plus, if you measure the size of your mugs and spoons at home, they can double as measuring tools. If your cooking plan requires a precise measuring spoon or two, at least you have avoided bringing the entire set.

Pie Irons

These heavy tools deserve special mention because they offer a way to cook sandwiches, pies, and more over an open fire. Though you're not likely to want the extra weight when backpacking, they make great additions to a paddling kitchen or a car-camping adventure. To use a pie iron, you place bread and fillings into the tool's cast iron or aluminum cooking compartment then fold over a duplicate compartment connected by a hinge. The whole contraption has two long handles so you can hold the tool in the fire to cook up golden-brown grilled cheese, pizza, delicious desserts, hamburgers, French toast, and more.

Paddling Extras

Backcountry paddling trips are great because you can bring everything but the kitchen sink. Weight is not as much of a factor when you're floating, so consider these extras:

- **Dutch oven:** Our favorite item to bring on backcountry paddling trips, a cast-iron Dutch oven is a game changer. Pineapple upside-down cake, lasagna, pizza, casseroles, and more are possible with this bad boy. For four people, an 8-inch Dutch oven with a lid is fine. For four to eight people, you will want a 10- or 12-inch model.
- **Extra pots and pans:** If you can fit an extra pot or pan, bring it; more vessels makes mixing smoother.
- **Dishwashing basin:** Bring a plastic dishwashing tub or two.

Pack a Dutch oven when you can afford the extra weight. Photo: Travis, Creative Commons on Flickr

PACKING YOUR FOOD

Packing up your food for a backpacking trip is not so simple as throwing everything into a backpack and heading off into the woods. Your food bag should be as small as possible and watertight. We always use a stuff-sack system for packing our food, no matter the length or the type of trip. Ingredients for each type of meal (breakfasts, lunches, dinners, drink mixes, snacks, and desserts) go into their own bag. By divvying meal types into separate bags, it will be easier to find what you're looking for—and to divide weight between group members' packs (unless you're going solo).

Lining each stuff sack with a plastic trash compactor bag before loading in the food will keep your edibles fresh and will prevent leaks in or out. After packing the food in the lined stuff sack, press all the air out of the sack, give the compactor bag several twists, and fold the tail down inside the stuff sack. This will make your food bag 100 percent waterproof.

If you know you will be experiencing bad weather or if your route involves river crossings or canyoneering, double the trash compactor bags for extra protection. Twist and seal each of the two compactor bags separately. There are few things that will ruin your trip faster than a sopping wet bag of food!

We have thrown our backpacks over waterfalls—truly!—while canyoneering in Arizona, and packed safe inside double-bagged stuff sacks, our food was still dry as dust when we got to camp.

Even when using a trash compactor bag to line a stuff sack, make sure all individual items are first packed in zippered storage bags for extra protection.

RESUPPLYING

The food planning methods we recommend in this book work best for two- to ten-day trips. After ten days, it becomes difficult, but not impossible, to carry all of your food with you. Here are your best options for dealing with a resupply on a longer expedition:

Resupply rendezvous: Arrange to have a friend or a family member meet you along your route to resupply you with fresh food. This is a great opportunity to stock up on fresh ingredients; be sure to have them bring you steaks or something equally indulgent (and perishable) for that first dinner.

Cache: Before you leave, hide your food in a secure, weatherproof location along your route. Make sure you have permission from the landowner, that your spot is well hidden, and that it's safe from animals! The worst thing that

Next step: getting all of this into trash compactor bags and then stuff sacks. Photo: J Brew, Creative Commons on Flickr

could happen is if someone or something finds your stash and disturbs it—or takes the resupply you're counting on for survival. See "Keeping Your Food Safe from Animals," page 41, for more on preventing wildlife from inspecting your food supply.

Mail drops: People thru-hiking the Appalachian Trail or tackling other long-distance treks will often set up a series of mail drops for themselves. This option takes considerable planning but can be effective if your route regularly passes through towns and your schedule is reliable. Always contact the post offices in advance to make sure they will store your package for you.

Hike out and go to a store! This is always an option if it doesn't require detouring from your route. A store visit also gives you the chance to stock up on fresh ingredients.

A makeshift counter keeps your backcountry kitchen off the ground. Photo: Travis, Creative Commons on Flickr

ON THE TRAIL

CAMP KITCHEN

Most backcountry camp kitchens are very primitive. You will be cooking on the ground, so get used to it. Occasionally you may find a campsite with a picnic table, but don't count on it.

If you are at an established campsite, use whatever space is already impacted there for your kitchen. If you're camping in an unestablished campsite, look for rock, gravel, or sandy areas to reduce your overall impact. If you can find an open rock ledge, that is your best bet, and you'll leave virtually no impact.

If you are in active grizzly bear country, you'll want to set up your kitchen at least 100 yards away from where you'll be sleeping so you don't get a midnight visitor to your tent who smells the delicious Gado Gado pasta you were cooking nearby earlier.

If you're not in grizzly bear country, it's fairly typical to cook right in your campsite, but *never in your tent,* even if the weather is bad. Carbon monoxide fumes from your stove can sicken or even kill you. You also don't want to risk spilling hot water, grease, or other food where you'll be sleeping!

Try to set up your camp kitchen with all of your ingredients, pots and pans, and stove laid out in a neat semicircle around whoever is cooking. Gather all meal-specific stuff sacks in your camp kitchen as soon as you arrive in camp. That way you can simply reach for ingredients and tools and don't have to get up dozens of times to root around in four different backpacks to find what you're looking for.

If you're expecting bad weather or are going to be in the same camp for more than one night, put a tarp over your kitchen to protect you from sun and/or rain. To properly pitch a tarp, you'll need to know two knots: the bowline and the trucker's hitch. Read more about these knots in AMC's *Mountain Skills Manual.* Find two stout trees and pitch the tarp as tightly as you can. A loose tarp not only exhibits bad style, but it won't keep out the elements. Hiking poles or downed branches can serve as posts to raise the edges up a little for entry and exit.

LEAVE NO TRACE

Center for Outdoor Ethics | LNT.org

All backcountry visitors should strive to minimize their impact on the land and to leave no trace of their visit. Not only will the wildlife benefit, but the next human visitor to your campsite won't even know you were there. Here are the guidelines to creating a true Leave No Trace (LNT) kitchen:

- **Set up on a hard surface.** Rock is best, followed by sand or crushed rock. At all costs, try to avoid trampling vegetation. Use established camping sites and campsite paths.
- **Carry in, carry out.** All trash you bring with you should leave with you. This includes food scraps and leftovers, including the food scraps from your dishwashing. Store leftovers in a sealable plastic container for use the next day. Scrape any leftovers you don't plan to eat into a zippered storage bag and carry it out with you.
- **Whenever possible, use a stove.** Even in areas where fire is permitted, a stove affects the surrounding area minimally.
- **Be smart if you choose to cook on a fire.** Only light fires in permitted areas and always use established fire rings.
- **Used downed wood only.** Never cut wood from a standing tree for firewood.
- **Discard dishwater using the dilute-and-disperse method.** Use a small amount of soap to clean your dishes. Filter food scraps out of dishwater with a small piece of window screen. Spread the remaining dishwater out over as large an area as possible.

COOKING SAFETY IN THE BACKCOUNTRY

Cooking safety in the backcountry is pretty similar to being at home, with one major difference: you are miles from help if you need it. The sheer isolation and difficulty of getting help in case of an injury or accident in the kitchen should make all backcountry chefs more vigilant.

Boiling water is one of the most dangerous parts of a backcountry trip. Your chance of having to evacuate due to scalding is higher than that of getting bitten by a snake or being attacked by a bear. To avoid burns, always follow this advice:

- Never reach across a stove. You stand a good chance of knocking it over.
- Anyone cooking or assisting in the kitchen area should be wearing the most protective footwear they have available—usually hiking boots. This creates

Never, ever reach across a stove. Photo: Travis, Creative Commons on Flickr

the awareness that you are at risk and helps protect your feet from burns.

- Use your best judgment when involving kids in helping with the cooking. You know them best and what they're capable of.
- When pouring water for hot brew, set the pot on the ground and use a cup to ladle the water out. Don't pour the water straight from the pot into a mug.
- Keep little ones away from the stove, particularly when boiling water.
- Never leave a lit stove unattended.
- Cut on a cutting board that's on a hard, stable surface, not on your leg or in your hand.
- Keep knives in their sheaths when not in use. You can make a quick and easy sheath with some cardboard and duct tape.
- If you're cooking over a fire, keep a bucket of water handy. Wind gusts can blow embers into dry leaves, and if that happens, you've got a problem on your hands. You don't want to waste precious time running to get water.
- If a small stove fire does erupt, smother it with dirt, a sleeping bag, a blanket, or clothing. Never throw water on a gas or oil fire. Doing so will cause the fire to spread.

COOKING OVER FIRE

Fire is by far the oldest and most time-tested method of backcountry cooking. Fire has many advantages: You don't have to carry a stove or fuel, and fire provides both warmth and a social gathering point. Most of the recipes in this book can be cooked right over a fire.

Remember that many backcountry locations don't permit fires or do not have established fire rings where you can cook. If that's the case on your chosen route, stick to using a stove. If you can light a fire along your route and will have access to a fire ring, here's how you can cook safely and efficiently.

First, place two flat rocks in the fire pit, leaving a 6- to 10-inch gap between the rocks. You want this gap to be small enough that the rocks will hold your pots and pans, but large enough to allow a large portion of the cooking vessels exposed to the coals. Next build a fire and wait for it to reduce to a pile of red-hot coals. Coals are much easier to cook over than actively burning wood, which is difficult to regulate. If you need to build up some immediate heat mid-prep, throw some small pieces of wood onto the coals, but nothing larger than 1.5 inches in diameter. If the coals get too hot and food starts to burn, push some of the coals aside.

The fire and smoke will darken your pots and pans, so don't use anything you don't mind turning black.

Many backcountry travelers use lightweight metal grates that span between rocks on the edge of the fire to create a uniform, level cooking surface for pots and pans. This grate can be as simple as two metal rods, or an ultra-light metal mesh surface that doubles as a backcountry grill for fresh meats and fish. While most big-box retailers carry simple and lightweight camp-fire grills or grates, the gold-standard model is from Purcell Trench, which makes custom grates for the back-country that come with a fabric sleeve to keep the rest of your gear clean.

If you're planning to cook on a fire, weather can be an issue. If it is rainy out, it can be challenging to find dry wood to get your meal going. Birch bark from downed logs (*never from living trees*) will burn in almost any condition, as it is full of flammable oils. You may also want to bring a fire starter. You can buy small bricks of sawdust

Only use dead and downed wood to build a fire. Photo: Brianna Murphy/AMC Photo Contest

soaked in paraffin or make your own by dipping cotton balls in melted paraffin before you leave home. For more detailed information on LNT-friendly fire-starting in the backcountry, check out AMC's *Mountain Skills Manual.*

OTHER COOKING METHODS

You might have arrived at this book assuming you'd be sautéing, frying, boiling, and rehydrating every meal, and while you'll look to those methods for plenty of show-stopping dishes, you might even get really adventurous and try backcountry baking—and beyond.

Imagine hiking to a remote ridge and setting up camp on a rocky ledge with views to the west. After setting up camp, you start a small fire in the fire pit, mix and knead your home-prepped dough, and bake a fresh loaf of bread. As you sit on the ledge and watch the sunset, you enjoy a steaming golden-brown roll, drenched in real melted butter and slathered in honey that drips off the edges. Heaven!

Reflector Ovens

Lightweight and compact, these are great for paddling, cycling, and back-packing trips. Reflector ovens are basically a square metal box that has been cut in half, with a shelf in the middle to hold a baking pan. The oven folds up to about the size of a three-ring binder and weighs as little as 1 pound. They are generally available at larger outdoor retailers, as well as online, but there are plenty of DIY videos online to help you make your own—some-times even lighter weight than those commercially available. We use a Sproul Baker, which weighs in at 2 pounds, complete with the baking pan. Even though 2 pounds sounds heavy for backpacking, consider this: A typical liquid fuel backpacking stove weighs about 15 ounces, along with a fuel bottle that weighs 5 ounce; factor in 20 ounces of fuel for a grand total of 40 ounces, or 2.5 pounds. Plus, a reflector oven can make cookies.

To use a reflector oven, simply build a small- to medium-sized fire. The fire should be about as wide and high as the opening of your oven. The radiating heat of the fire will bounce off the metal walls of the oven and get redirected to the food.

Once your fire is going, place the oven 4 to 8 inches away from the flames. Turn the food every 15 minutes or so to ensure even cooking. If the food looks like it's burning, move the oven farther from the flames. If the food is cooking

A reflector oven traps the radiating heat from a nearby fire. Photo: Ethan Hipple

too slowly or not cooking at all, either build your flames up or move the oven closer to the flames. There will be some trial and error; it's not an exact science. But even beginner backcountry chefs will be able to produce some delicious baked goods.

Dutch Ovens

Dutch ovens are perhaps our favorite backcountry cooking device. They make delicious cakes, rolls, bread, lasagna, pizza, and calzones. They are, however, heavy. *Quite* heavy. While Dutch ovens are not feasible for backpacking, we always stick one in the car to use while car camping near the trailhead on the first or last night of the trip. And a rafting or kayaking trip would not be complete without at least one real lasagna dinner and pineapple upside-down cake!

The best Dutch ovens in the backcountry are cast iron pots with a flanged lid that has a raised lip. The lid is designed to hold hot coals on the top, cooking the food from above. If your Dutch oven doesn't have a raised lip, you won't be able to hold heat on the top of the oven, so be sure to buy a model that has this feature. The pot usually has small legs that hold it off the ground so you can slide some coals underneath, cooking from the bottom at the same time. Because you are cooking from the top and bottom simultaneously, this pot becomes an oven.

Dutch ovens are available almost everywhere: big-box stores, sporting goods stores, outdoor retailers, and online. Remember: The models without the raised lip or flanged lid are designed for baking inside a conventional oven and will make it extremely difficult to hold in your coals.

To use your Dutch oven, start by building a fire and letting it burn down to red-hot coals. Alternatively, you can use charcoal briquettes, which have a very consistent and long-lasting heat. Push the coals over to one side of the fire pit and use the cleared side for cooking. Make a small pile of red-hot coals (or 8 to 10 briquettes) and lower the Dutch oven down over the coals. The coals are your bottom heat source. In general, keep the bottom heat about one-third the strength of the top heat. It is easy to burn the bottom of your dish, so be conservative with your bottom heat until you get the hang of it.

Make sure the oven lid is on tight and add your top heat: a solid, single layer of briquettes or a nice, 2-inch-thick layer of red-hot coals. If you use briquettes, they will last the entire cooking time. If you use hot coals, you will have to replenish them (on bottom and top) as they die out and cool off.

A heavy, long handled metal spoon is very helpful for moving the coals and briquettes around. A pair of pliers is also helpful for picking up the hot handle and the hot lid.

Dutch ovens cook from above and below when surrounded by coals. Photo: Travis, Creative Commons on Flickr

Bake your dish, trying not to open the lid too often. Once the top is golden brown, it is most likely done. Test it with a knife or fork then take it off the fire. Because the thick cast iron is so hot when you take it off, the dish will continue to cook for another five to ten minutes after you remove it from the coals.

Fry-Bake Pans

These lightweight backpacking pans are specifically designed for frying and baking in the backcountry. They are basically a modern-day, lightweight Dutch oven. They are light as a feather (about 10 ounces), compact, and time-tested. They can be used to prepare most of the recipes in this book and are designed to be used over a standard backpacking stove that generates bottom heat. They have a flanged lid with a lip that accommodates coals, briquettes, or a small "twiggy fire" on top to produce top heat for baking. They are available at larger outdoor retailers or online. Banks Fry-Bake invented and still sells these great backcountry kitchen staples.

To use a fry-bake pan, set your stove to simmer-level heat or as low as it will go. Place the fry-bake pan over the stove and put the lid on. Build a small "twiggy fire" on top. A twiggy fire is a fire made up of dead-and-downed pieces of wood no bigger than a pencil. This fire will burn hot and quickly, so make sure you gather a good supply of downed twigs and branches beforehand. You can also just put coals from a fire directly on the lid and keep adding them as you cook. Remember to follow any guidelines for building a fire in the area where you're camping.

You can also use a fry-bake pan like a Dutch oven: in a fire pit, with coals below the pan and on top. However you choose to use it, monitor the heat and check the contents often with your nose and your eyes to make sure the food isn't burning.

A Note on Cooking Fish

There is nothing quite like catching your own dinner in a mountain stream or lake. Whether you're fishing for rainbows, brook trout, or salmon, there are lots of great ways to cook and enjoy your backcountry feast. We don't plan on having fish as our primary food source, because there's always the chance you won't catch anything. But fish can be a great supplement to your meals, and fishing is a great way to spend some time in the backcountry. If you don't have experience gutting and filleting fish, go fishing with someone who does, or watch some videos online. Practice makes perfect.

How you prepare and cook the fish depends on your personal taste. Many people prefer their fish cooked whole, with skin, head, and tail intact. Others prefer to fillet the fish and leave the skin on. Still others go the extra step and fillet the fish then remove the skin, leaving delicious fish cutlets.

While filleting a raw fish will remove most of the bones, you likely will have some left to pick out while eating. For this reason, some people cook fish with the bones and skin intact; it can be easier to pull flaky, cooked meat off the bone. Always pack out any bones with the rest of your trash.

KEEPING FOOD SAFE FROM ANIMALS

It's crucial that you take precautions to protect your supplies from curious and hungry animals. This can be an issue in bear country as easily as any-where else. You don't want to wake up to a bear in your tent, but you don't want to wake up to a chipmunk polishing off the last of your pancake mix, either. Don't rely on your lined stuff sacks or your backpack to discourage animals of any size from investigating your food. They can and will smell it.

A bear canister—a packable metal can in which you can carry your food—may work for some people, but you will be constrained by the size of can you're willing to carry.

Use paracord to hang your bear-proof bag 15 feet off the ground. Photo: Joan Terzo/AMC Photo Contest

Some established campsites offer sturdy metal boxes in which you can stow your food whenever you're not cooking. On busy weekends at popular campsites, the boxes may fill up very fast.

To be sure you keep your food safe, plan on hanging it in a tree using the following method.

- Take a long piece of parachute cord (at least 50 feet).
- Tie a weight on the end; rocks or a large carabiner work well. Make sure the cord is loosely coiled on the ground, or it will get tangled as you throw the heavy end.
- Pitch the heavy end over a branch at least 15 feet high.
- Make sure the cord passes over the branch at least 5 feet away from the tree trunk. Otherwise, an animal may be able to climb the tree and swipe to catch the bag hanging next to the trunk.
- Lower the heavy end back down to the ground, keeping the remainder of the cord draped over the branch. This is the end you will use to raise the bags up.
- Untie the rock and tie a bowline knot on the end of the cord.
- Use a carabiner to clip together your stuff sacks of food.
- Clip the carabiner around the length of cord that you will be pulling on to raise it. This will keep everything contained as you pull it up.
- Hoist it all up at least 15 feet off the ground. Secure the loose end to a nearby tree or rock.

WATER TREATMENT METHODS

In the backcountry, you must treat all drinking water to avoid waterborne illnesses, such as giardiasis and exposure to other contaminants. Unless your cooking method brings all water to a rolling boil, use treated water in all food and drinks. *(Note: For dishwashing, there is no need to purify rinse water, as long as the dishes dry completely before the next use. The organisms can't survive without water.)* For more information, see "Appendix B: Drinking Water Treatment Methods," page 221. For a comprehensive review of water treatment, see *AMC's Mountain Skills Manual.*

A hand pump effectively filters water. Photo: Deborah Lee Soltesz, Creative Commons on Flickr

DISHWASHING

We have tried to plan the recipes in this book to require as few dishes as possible. No matter how hard you try, however, you will have to do dishes in the backcountry.

Many minimalist campers simply grab a handful of sand or fine gravel, add a splash of water, and scrub their dishes out. Toss the dishwater and sand out 100 feet away from any water source, distributing it across a broad area so no one plant takes the brunt. Rinse the dish well and put it on a rock to dry.

That said, washing with hot water, soap, and a proper rinse will get your dishes cleaner, killing germs and grime that can cause backcountry illnesses. We highly recommend doing a full wash for proper backcountry hygiene. Plus, it's another chance to get your hands truly clean!

- Before you start eating your hot meal, put water on the stove or fire to heat.
- After the water is hot (but not boiling), add soap.
- Scrape all dishes into your zippered storage bag of trash, getting them as clean as possible before you wash in the water. You don't want the dishwater getting nasty and greasy after the first dirty dish.
- Scrub dishes in the hot soapy water then set them aside on a rock or pine needles.
- If you have another spare pot, fill it with water (can be untreated) and rinse the dishes.
- If you don't have a clean pot for rinse water, wash all of the dishes and set them aside in a pile. Drain the water from the wash pot, refill it with rinse water, and rinse all of your dishes.
- Let dishes dry on a rock ledge, pine needles, or in a dish hammock hung between two trees.
- Use a 5-by-5-inch piece of screen to capture any food scraps then add these to your zipped storage bag of trash. Disperse the dirty dishwater widely, 100 feet away from water sources.
- Be sure to give your wash pot a final rinse and set it out to dry.

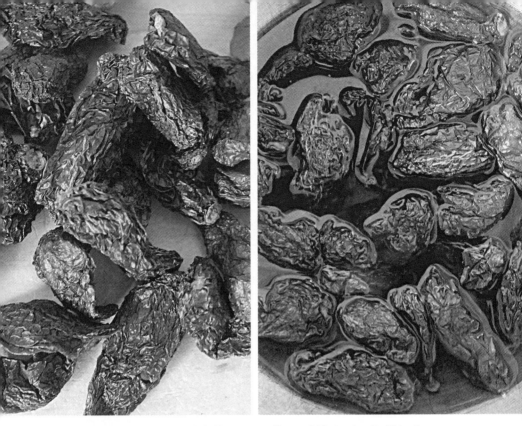

To rehydrate dried peppers, cover them in boiling water and let stand. Photos: Jennifer Wehunt

REHYDRATION

Unless specified otherwise in a recipe, most dehydrated foods rehydrate with a 1:1 ratio of dried food to water. The basic method is as follows:

- In a pot, measure out one part dried ingredients to one part water.
- Soak dried food in cold water for 5 to 10 minutes.
- Turn on heat and bring to a boil for 1 minute.
- Turn off heat, keep lid on, and let cool for 10 minutes.
- Insulate the pot if possible. You can make a pot cozy out of an old foam camping-mattress pad or buy a commercially available cozy.

SECTION 4
BREAKFAST

Breakfast has long been an afterthought of backcountry cooking. Hikers, paddlers, and cyclists crawl out of the tent; throw hot water on some pre-packaged, artificially flavored oatmeal; and pack up camp. But no longer! Don't subject yourself to the saccharine-sweet, empty calories of prepackaged breakfasts. The fake flavor and mushy texture will do little to beat back the dark pall of a rainy morning or the nerves over a long day ahead.

You don't need to settle for a mediocre existence. A real breakfast recalls the distant taste of home, the smell of Mom's cooking, a memory of wholesome goodness. Breakfast should be delicious, hearty, even joyous! Start your day in the backcountry with fresh, fry-baked skillet muffins; pancakes with crispy, buttery edges; homemade granola; cheesy omelets; spicy huevos rancheros; and real steel-cut oatmeal, with wholesome toppings.

Your days of sad, instant trail breakfasts are over. Welcome to a new world of wholesome, quick, and delicious breakfasts.

Photo: Jennifer Wehunt

COFFEE

Basic Coffee Methods

Coffee deserves special mention here. In all of our adventures, from the craggy ridges of the White Mountains to the peaks of the Rockies to the depths of the Amazonian rainforest, we have always figured out a way to prepare a good cup of coffee in the morning—and usually at night, as well. Here are some of our many methods for making coffee in the backcountry. We've tried them all at one point or another, and we've even resorted to grinding whole coffee beans between two rocks when someone mistakenly bought beans on a trip. For the truly devoted, nothing will get in the way of that fresh cup of Joe. Where there is a will, there is a way.

A French press isn't the lightest option, but it works in the wild. Photo: Travis, Creative Commons on Flickr

FRENCH PRESS

There are many brands of lightweight French presses appropriate for the backcountry. The French press is one of the heavier options out there, and they can be quite expensive, as well. You can even get a French press that fits right in your mug.

DRIP

Most grocery stores sell single-serving plastic drip cones that you can use with single-serve filters and regular ground coffee to make a great cup of drip coffee. Just heat up water, pour it over the grounds, through the filter, and let it drip into your mug, gravity-style.

PERCOLATORS

Old-school camping percolators are great for rafting and paddling trips, but they're pretty heavy for backpacking. They can be found in enamel or stainless steel in most outdoor outfitters or even big-box stores.

COWBOY COFFEE

The simplest and cheapest option. Simply throw a couple of tablespoons of ground coffee into your mug, pour in hot water, and let it sit for 10 minutes. The grounds will eventually sink, leaving you with delicious coffee that gets stronger and stronger the closer you get to the bottom. Eventually, though, you'll just be sucking up grounds, so stop and discard the waste before you get to the bottom of your mug. This method works best if you drink your coffee black, as stirring in milk and sugar disturbs the grounds again and you end up waiting a long time for them to settle back down.

For a no-frills version, go cowboy: ground coffee plus hot water. Photo: Alan Levine, Creative Commons on Flickr

GRANOLAS AND BREAKFAST BARS

··

Basic Granola Method

Serves: 6

All of the granola variations in this book follow the same basic instructions. Once you've tried a few, experiment with your own combinations.

Lots of people file granola under "breakfast," but it can fit in almost any part of your day on the trail. Eat it on its own, put it in your favorite trail mix, or think of it as a side for your breakfast entrées. Although you *could* buy ready-made granola at the store, easy, delicious, wholesome granola made at home is far and away the way to go. There is no limit to the different varieties you can come up with. Create your own magic blend with your favorite nuts, dried fruits, and spices. If you aren't feeling creative, follow one of these tried-and-true recipes.

METHOD

1. Preheat the oven to 300° F. Grease a large baking sheet.
2. In a large bowl, combine liquid ingredients, sugar, and spices. Whisk until smooth. (If using coconut oil, melt on the stove or in a microwave until it becomes a liquid.)
3. Combine dry ingredients in a smaller bowl, including oats, seeds, raw (unroasted) nuts, and/or coconut. Do not mix in dried fruit or roasted nuts at this time.
4. Stir dry ingredients into liquid ingredients until well combined.
5. Spread mixture onto a greased baking sheet and bake for 30 to 45 minutes, or until golden brown and fragrant.
6. Remove from oven and let cool for several hours on baking sheet.
7. Gently stir in dried fruit and roasted nuts. Be careful to leave some chunks of granola unbroken.
8. Store in a zippered storage bag or any airtight container.

Coconut Cashew Granola

Serves: 6 | **Weight: 1.4 lbs.** | V | V+ | DF | GF

INGREDIENTS

¼ cup maple syrup

¼ cup coconut oil

¼ cup dark brown sugar

1 teaspoon salt

3 cups rolled oats

¾ cup shredded coconut (check labels and choose an unsweetened, single-ingredient version)

1 cup cashew chunks

Servings	6
PER SERVING	
Calories	543
Fat	31g
Protein	12g
Sodium	405mg
Fiber	6g
Carbohydrates	58g
Sugar	20g
Vitamin A 0% • Vitamin C 1%	
Calcium 5% • Iron 26%	

METHOD

Prepare as directed in Basic Granola Method, page 50.

Homemade granola has fewer preservatives than store-bought. Photo: Travis, Creative Commons on Flickr

Cranberry Nut Granola

Serves: 6 | **Weight: 2.2 lbs.** | V | DF

INGREDIENTS

½ cup vegetable oil
2 tablespoons maple syrup
½ cup honey
1 teaspoon salt
2 tablespoons brown sugar
2 teaspoons cinnamon
2 teaspoons vanilla extract
4 cups rolled oats
¾ cup wheat germ
¾ cup oat bran
1 cup dried cranberries
½ cup slivered almonds
½ cup chopped walnuts

Servings	6
PER SERVING	
Calories	**744**
Fat	**34g**
Protein	**16g**
Sodium	**403mg**
Fiber	**12g**
Carbohydrates	**105g**
Sugar	**46g**
Vitamin A: 0% • Vitamin C: 1%	
Calcium: 9% • Iron: 27%	

METHOD

Prepare as directed in Basic Granola Method, page 50.

Almond Sesame Mango Granola

Serves: 6 | **Weight: 1.7 lbs.** | V | V+ | DF | GF

INGREDIENTS

⅓ cup coconut oil
½ cup maple syrup
¼ cup brown sugar
1 teaspoon almond extract
1 teaspoon salt
3 cups rolled oats
½ cup raw sesame seeds
1 cup dried mangos, chopped
1 cup slivered almonds

Servings	6
PER SERVING	
Calories	**540**
Fat	29g
Protein	11g
Sodium	402mg
Fiber	8g
Carbohydrates	65g
Sugar	30g
Vitamin A: 4% • Vitamin C: 13%	
Calcium: 21% • Iron: 25%	

METHOD

Prepare as directed in Basic Granola Method, page 50.

Pistachio Apricot Granola

Serves: 6 | **Weight: 2.2 lbs.** | V V+ DF GF

INGREDIENTS

½ cup maple syrup
⅓ cup coconut oil
¼ cup brown sugar
1 teaspoon salt
1 teaspoon cardamom
3 cups rolled oats
1 cup raw pepitas (pumpkin seeds)
1 cup shredded coconut (check labels and choose an unsweetened, single-ingredient version)
1½ cups pistachio nuts (shelled)
1 cup dried apricots

Servings	6
PER SERVING	
Calories	**764**
Fat	45g
Protein	20g
Sodium	407mg
Fiber	12g
Carbohydrates	81g
Sugar	40g
Vitamin A: 18% • Vitamin C: 5%	
Calcium: 10% • Iron: 35%	

METHOD

Prepare as directed in Basic Granola Method, page 50.

There are as many ways to garnish your granola as there are trees in the woods. Photo: Ryan Smith

Dark Chocolate Coconut Granola

Serves: 6 | **Weight: 1 lb.** |

INGREDIENTS

⅓ cup coconut oil

¼ cup maple syrup

½ teaspoon vanilla extract

5 tablespoons turbinado sugar, divided

⅛ teaspoon salt

¼ cup cocoa powder

½ cup rolled oats

½ cup shredded coconut (check labels and choose an
   unsweetened, single-ingredient version)

1 cup semisweet chocolate chips

¾ cup slivered almonds

Coarse sea salt to taste

Servings	6
PER SERVING	
Calories	**500**
Fat	31g
Protein	6g
Sodium	54mg
Fiber	6g
Carbohydrates	54g
Sugar	39g
Vitamin A: 1% • Vitamin C: 0%	
Calcium: 6% • Iron: 15%	

METHOD

1. Prepare dry and wet ingredients as directed in Basic Granola Method
   up through baking, step 5. When combining liquid ingredients and
   sugar, use 3 tablespoons of turbinado sugar, reserving 2 tablespoons
   for topping.

2. Once granola is done baking, remove pan from the oven and sprinkle with
   chocolate chips and almonds.

3. Return pan to oven for 1 minute to soften the chocolate.

4. Remove pan from the oven again and sprinkle with remaining 2
   tablespoons of turbinado sugar and sea salt to taste.

5. Let granola cool on pan for several hours without stirring. This ensures
   that you don't break up all of the granola clusters.

Peanut Butter Banana Breakfast Bars

Makes: 12 bars | **Weight: 2.2 lbs.** | V DF GF

These protein- and fiber-rich bars are a great breakfast option when you want an early start. Just grab one of these and hit the trail.

Servings	6
PER SERVING	
Calories	292
Fat	17g
Protein	10g
Sodium	200mg
Fiber	6g
Carbohydrates	29g
Sugar	12g
Vitamin A: 0% • Vitamin C: 4%	
Calcium: 5% • Iron: 9%	

INGREDIENTS
3 ripe bananas (the riper, the better)
1 cup peanut butter
¼ cup honey
1½ teaspoons cinnamon
½ teaspoon salt
2 teaspoons vanilla extract
¼ cup ground flax seed
2 cups rolled oats
1 cup slivered almonds

METHOD
1. Preheat oven to 350° F and line an 8-by-8-inch baking pan with parchment paper.
2. Mash bananas together with peanut butter, honey, cinnamon, salt, vanilla extract, and flax seeds. Stir until smooth with a hand mixer or a standing mixer.
3. Stir in oats and almonds until fully incorporated. Spread into prepared baking pan.
4. Bake for 30 minutes, or until edges turn golden brown and center sets up.
5. Let cool in the pan before cutting into bars, wrap in plastic wrap, and store in a cool place.

MUFFINS

Basic Skillet Muffin Mix and Method

| Makes: 6 muffins | Weight: 0.8 lbs. | | | |

Skillet muffins are a great treat on the trail. There are endless varieties that you can make, depending on your creativity, and you can incorporate any type of dried fruit, nut, or seed into this basic recipe.

Before you leave home, mix up the dry ingredients for each muffin batch in separate bags so that all you have to do in camp is dump the dry mix in a bowl and add the wet ingredients before baking. Label the bags with a permanent marker so you know what to add to which mix.

There are several ways to cook skillet muffins. Use the ingredients and method below as a starting point for the variations that follow—or for your own creations.

Servings	6
PER SERVING	
Calories	279
Fat	10g
Protein	6g
Sodium	469mg
Fiber	1g
Carbohydrates	41g
Sugar	8g
Vitamin A: 6% • Vitamin C: 1%	
Calcium: 10% • Iron: 35%	

INGREDIENTS

2 cups flour
1 tablespoon baking powder
½ teaspoon salt
3 tablespoons sugar
4 tablespoons powdered milk
4 tablespoons butter powder or melted butter
2 tablespoons egg crystals
1 cup plus 6 tablespoons water

Plan ahead and measure out your skillet muffin ingredients at home. Photo: Sarah Hipple

METHOD

1. Grease a fry-bake pan, Dutch oven, reflector oven pan, or frying pan. Preheat oven or frying pan over a low flame.
2. Mix everything together in a bowl. Add water then stir batter just enough to incorporate liquid. Small lumps in batter, pea size or smaller, are OK.
3. Spoon golf ball-sized dollops of batter onto prepared pan.
4. *If using a fry-bake pan, Dutch oven, or reflector oven:* Bake for 15 to 20 minutes.
5. *If using a frying pan:* Put pan over low flame and cover. Cook for 8 to 9 minutes, then flip and cook for another 8 to 9 minutes.
6. Keep a close eye on the heat, as the muffins can burn easily. Cooking at a lower heat for a little longer is best.
7. Muffins are done when tops don't appear wet, are golden brown, and spring back slightly to the touch.

Donut Skillet Muffins

Don't make these on a morning when you're trying to get out of camp early. We prefer to take our time. Make some hot brew, enjoy the view, and indulge in these sweet, buttery delights. Also make sure you wash your hands especially well, as you will want to lick each finger clean! You could bag the cinnamon and sugar ahead of time, separate from the basic mix.

Servings	6
PER SERVING	
Calories	381
Fat	18g
Protein	6g
Sodium	469mg
Fiber	1g
Carbohydrates	49g
Sugar	16g
Vitamin A: 11% • Vitamin C: 1%	
Calcium: 21% • Iron: 13%	

INGREDIENTS
Basic Skillet Muffin Mix, page 56
½ teaspoon nutmeg
4 tablespoons butter (in addition to basic mix; fresh is better than dried here)
1 teaspoon cinnamon
4 tablespoons sugar (in addition to basic mix)

METHOD
1. Grease a fry-bake pan, Dutch oven, reflector oven pan, or frying pan. Preheat oven or frying pan on a low flame.

2. Prepare Basic Skillet Muffin Mix and add nutmeg. Cook as directed in Basic Skillet Muffin.

3. Remove fully cooked muffins from pan.

4. When pan is empty but still hot, add butter to pan.

5. While butter is melting, mix cinnamon and sugar together in a separate bowl.

6. Roll each muffin in the melted butter, coating all sides. Immediately roll buttery muffins in cinnamon sugar.

Blueberry Skillet Muffins

This is a great choice when you have the opportunity to pick some blueberries around your campsite or along the trail.

Servings	6
PER SERVING	
Calories	380
Fat	18g
Protein	6g
Sodium	470mg
Fiber	1g
Carbohydrates	50g
Sugar	16g
Vitamin A: 11% • Vitamin C: 1%	
Calcium: 21% • Iron: 13%	

INGREDIENTS

Basic Skillet Muffin Mix, page 56
Up to 1½ cups blueberries
1 teaspoon cinnamon, divided
2 tablespoons sugar (in addition to basic mix)

METHOD

1. Grease a fry-bake pan, Dutch oven, reflector oven pan, or frying pan. Preheat oven or frying pan over a low flame.

2. Prepare Basic Skillet Muffin Mix as directed, adding ½ teaspoon cinnamon to dry ingredients. Fold in blueberries.

3. Mix up remaining ½ teaspoon cinnamon with sugar in a separate bowl.

4. Spoon batter into prepared pan.

5. Top batter generously with cinnamon sugar. Continue baking as in Basic Skillet Muffins method, page 57.

Full of antioxidants, blueberries make a great muffin add-in—if you can wait until breakfast.
Photo: Jennifer Wehunt

Cranberry Orange Skillet Muffins

Makes: 6 muffins | **Weight: 1 lb** | V

INGREDIENTS

Basic Skillet Muffin Mix, page 56
1 teaspoon orange juice powder
1 teaspoon orange zest
1 cup dried cranberries
½ teaspoon cinnamon
2 tablespoons sugar

Servings	6
PER SERVING	
Calories	380
Protein	6g
Sodium	470mg
Fiber	2g
Carbohydrates	62g
Sugar	26g
Vitamin A: 6% • Vitamin C: 4%	
Calcium: 21% • Iron: 14%	

METHOD

1. Grease a fry-bake pan, Dutch oven, reflector oven pan, or frying pan. Preheat oven or frying pan on a low flame.
2. Prepare Basic Skillet Muffin Mix, adding orange juice powder and orange zest with dry ingredients. Fold in dried cranberries.
3. Mix cinnamon and sugar in a separate bowl.
4. Spoon batter into prepared pan.
5. Top batter generously with cinnamon sugar. Continue baking as in Basic Skillet Muffins method, page 57.

Morning Glory Skillet Muffins

Makes: 6 muffins | **Weight: 1.5 lbs.** | V

INGREDIENTS

Basic Skillet Muffin Mix, page 56
1 teaspoon cinnamon
½ cup shredded, unsweetened coconut
½ cup chopped walnuts
1 cup raisins
2 carrots, shredded

Servings	6
PER SERVING	
Calories	450
Fat	19g
Protein	9g
Sodium	490mg
Fiber	4g
Carbohydrates	64g
Sugar	24g
Vitamin A: 86% • Vitamin C: 5%	
Calcium: 24% • Iron: 18%	

METHOD

1. Grease a fry-bake pan, Dutch oven, reflector oven pan, or frying pan. Preheat oven or frying pan on a low flame.
2. Prepare Basic Skillet Muffin Mix, adding cinnamon, coconut, and walnuts to dry ingredients. Fold in raisins and shredded carrots.
3. Cook as directed in Basic Skillet Muffins, page 57.

PANCAKES

Basic Pancake (Caker) Mix and Method

| Serves: 4 to 6 | Weight: 0.8 lbs. | V | NF | |

In the backcountry kitchens of Appalachian Mountain Club huts, we call these "cakers." It just rolls off the tongue. Try it: cakers!

There are countless things you can put in, or on top of, your cakers. Batter additions include flax seeds, chocolate chips, berries, toffee chips, or sliced bananas. Top your cakers with maple syrup, honey, homemade syrup (recipe follows), applesauce, chocolate hazelnut spread, cashew or peanut butter, or cinnamon sugar.

Servings	6
PER SERVING	
Calories	218
Fat	10g
Protein	7g
Sodium	471mg
Fiber	1g
Carbohydrates	41g
Sugar	9g
Vitamin A: 6% • Vitamin C: 1%	
Calcium: 20% • Iron: 13%	

INGREDIENTS
2 cups flour
1 tablespoon baking powder
½ teaspoon salt
3 tablespoons sugar
4 tablespoons powdered milk
4 tablespoons butter powder or melted butter
2 tablespoons egg crystals
2 cups water, as needed

METHOD
1. Grease or butter a frying pan and heat over a medium-low flame.
2. Mix dry ingredients in a bowl. Add enough water and stir batter until it is slightly thicker than heavy cream. Start with less water and add until you reach a pourable consistency. The thicker the batter, the thicker the pancakes, and the longer they will take to cook.
3. Spoon small amounts of batter into greased or buttered frying pan. Making pancakes small will help when you are trying to flip them. We prefer many small pancakes with crispy edges.
4. Keep a close eye on heat. Cakers can burn easily, so aim for medium flame.
5. Pancakes are ready to flip when bubbles form on top, pop, and don't appear wet anymore.
6. Flip and cook for less time on second side.

Cornbread Cakers

INGREDIENTS
1⅓ cups flour
⅔ cup cornmeal
2 tablespoons sugar
4 teaspoons baking powder
1 teaspoon salt
4 tablespoons egg crystals
⅓ cup powdered milk
4 tablespoons butter powder or melted butter
2 cups water, as needed

Servings	4
PER SERVING	
Calories	450
Fat	17g
Protein	12g
Sodium	1154g
Fiber	2g
Carbohydrates	62g
Sugar	11g
Vitamin A: 13% • Vitamin C: 0%	
Calcium: 39% • Iron: 22%	

METHOD
Prepare as directed in Basic Pancake (Caker) Method, page 61.

Homemade Syrup

This syrup is a great substitute—by no means a replacement!—for maple syrup and is easy to whip up anywhere.

Servings	3
PER SERVING	
Calories	381
Fat	12g
Protein	0g
Sodium	24mg
Fiber	0g
Carbohydrates	72g
Sugar	71g
Vitamin A: 7% • Vitamin C: 0%	
Calcium: 7% • Iron: 3%	

INGREDIENTS
3 tablespoons fresh butter
1 cup brown sugar
½ cup water
⅛ teaspoon vanilla

METHOD
1. Melt butter and brown sugar in pan until smooth.
2. Pour in water and bring to a simmer. Reduce for 5 minutes, stirring frequently, until mixture starts to thicken.
3. As soon as sugar is dissolved, remove from heat and add vanilla.
4. Store in any watertight container.

The only thing that makes cakers even better?
Mix-ins, such as blueberries. Photo: Jennifer Wehunt

EGG DISHES

Basic Egg Scramble

| Serves: 4 | Weight: 0.3 lbs. | V | GF | NF | | |

Servings	4
PER SERVING	
Calories	173
Fat	13g
Protein	13g
Sodium	295mg
Fiber	0g
Carbohydrates	1g
Sugar	1g
Vitamin A: 12% • Vitamin C: 0%	
Calcium: 7% • Iron: 10%	

The advent of easy online shopping has changed backcountry cooking for the better. Specialty items like egg crystals were once the purview of high-end outdoor retailers and health food stores. Now they are available to anyone, anywhere—and at the click of a button, with two-day shipping! There are many brands available of varying quality. We used OvaEasy egg crystals when preparing the recipes for this book.

Egg scrambles are easy, and packed with protein and energy to keep you going strong all day on the trail. You can be very creative with what you put into your scramble. You might even decide to throw in the leftovers from last night's dinner. You can't go wrong as long as you have good ingredients. When you're on the trail and working hard, plan for two or even three servings of eggs per person.

Though nonstick frying pans can be a concern when used day in and day out at home, they are best for making eggs while camping. It can be a pain trying to clean stuck-on eggs from a regular stainless steel pan. Be sure to use butter or oil in the pan to minimize sticking.

If adding cheese to eggs, always add it *after* the eggs are done cooking. Adding cheese to raw eggs makes the cheese sweat; your eggs will get watery and gross.

Pro tip: Crack and store fresh eggs in a plastic bottle for easy transportation to backcountry destinations, such as AMC's High Cabin in New Hampshire, pictured above. Photo: Jennifer Wehunt

INGREDIENTS

1 tablespoon fresh butter
1 cup egg crystals
2 tablespoons powdered milk
¼ teaspoon salt
Pepper to taste
2 cups water

METHOD

1. Melt butter in pan over high flame.
2. Mix egg crystals and milk in a bowl with salt and pepper.
3. Add water.
4. Whisk until smooth.
5. Pour egg mixture into a hot, buttered pan and stir frequently, scraping the bottom of the pan until eggs are scrambled.
6. Remove from heat once all liquid is gone and eggs are fully cooked.

Denver Scramble

Serves: 4 | Weight: 1.3 lbs. | GF |

INGREDIENTS

Basic Egg Scramble, page 64
1 tablespoon fresh butter or oil (in addition to butter for Basic Egg Scramble)
½ cup diced onions
½ green pepper, chopped
½ cup chopped ham, salami, or dehydrated beef
1 cup sharp cheddar cheese, shredded

Servings	4
PER SERVING	
Calories	351
Fat	27g
Protein	24g
Sodium	696mg
Fiber	1g
Carbohydrates	4g
Sugar	2g
Vitamin A: 21% • Vitamin C: 22%	
Calcium: 28% • Iron: 12%	

METHOD

1. Heat 1 tablespoon butter or oil in a frying pan. Sauté onions and peppers until soft and starting to brown.

2. Add meat to vegetable mixture and continue to sauté for another minute.

3. Pour eggs over vegetables and meat and continue to cook as directed in Basic Egg Scramble.

4. Once egg mixture is cooked, add in the cheese. Stir to combine and let sit for a minute to allow cheese to melt.

Huevos Rancheros

True huevos rancheros are made with fried or poached eggs, but for the sake of making this dish backcountry-friendly, we make ours with an egg scramble. It's just as tasty and bound to give you plenty of energy to start your day.

Servings	4
PER SERVING	
Calories	409
Fat	24g
Protein	24g
Sodium	954mg
Fiber	4g
Carbohydrates	27g
Sugar	4g
Vitamin A: 21% • Vitamin C: 2%	
Calcium: 33% • Iron: 16%	

INGREDIENTS

Basic Egg Scramble, page 64
½ cup water (for reconstituting beans)
½ cup dried refried beans or 1 can pinto or black beans, drained
8 corn tortillas
½ to 1 cup sharp cheddar cheese, chopped or shredded (to taste)
1 cup salsa
⅛ teaspoon salt

METHOD

1. Heat ½ cup of water and reconstitute dried beans in a small bowl. Set aside.

2. Pan-fry corn tortillas in frying pan with a little bit of oil. Flip throughout cooking to get both sides golden brown. Set tortillas aside once crispy and sprinkle with salt.

3. Prepare and cook ingredients for Basic Egg Scramble, as directed.

4. Once eggs are cooked, cover with cheddar and remove from heat. Cover pan with a lid for 1 minute to let cheese melt.

5. To serve, put two tortillas in each bowl, cover with cheesy egg scramble, and pour salsa over top.

Eggs, cheese, and vegetables make a powerful fuel combo. Photo: Travis, Creative Commons on Flickr

Hash Brown and Bacon Scramble

Serves: 4 | **Weight: 0.6 lbs.** | GF | NF |

This scramble will give you plenty of power to get you started on your day: a classic breakfast, scrambled up in one pan!

INGREDIENTS

Basic Egg Scramble, page 64
1 cup dehydrated hash browns
1 cup boiling water
1 tablespoon fresh butter
6 slices precooked bacon, chopped
1 cup cheddar cheese, shredded

Servings	4
PER SERVING	
Calories	**511**
Fat	41g
Protein	25g
Sodium	767mg
Fiber	1g
Carbohydrates	11g
Sugar	4g
Vitamin A: 20% • Vitamin C: 7%	
Calcium: 28% • Iron: 15%	

METHOD

1. Cover dehydrated hash browns with boiling water and stir.
2. Cover with a tight-fitting lid and let sit for 10 minutes or until potatoes are soft.

3. Drain excess water from potatoes.

4. Heat butter in frying pan on medium flame then add hash browns and chopped bacon. Cook for several minutes until crispy and golden.

5. Prepare Basic Egg Scramble as directed on page 65, pouring egg mixture over crispy hot hash browns and bacon. Stir until eggs are fully cooked and remove from heat.

6. Stir in cheddar and serve.

Spinach, Mushroom, and Bacon Scramble

Serves: 4 · **Weight: 0.4 lbs.** · GF · NF ·

INGREDIENTS

Basic Egg Scramble, page 64
¼ cup dried mushrooms
1 cup boiling water
1 tablespoon fresh butter
6 slices precooked bacon, chopped
¼ cup dehydrated chopped spinach

Servings	4
PER SERVING	
Calories	355
Fat	31g
Protein	16g
Sodium	582mg
Fiber	0g
Carbohydrates	1g
Sugar	1g
Vitamin A: 18% • Vitamin C: 1%	
Calcium: 6% • Iron: 11%	

METHOD

1. Cover dehydrated mushrooms and spinach with boiling water and stir.

2. Cover with a tight-fitting lid and let sit for 10 minutes or until soft.

3. Drain excess water.

4. Heat butter in frying pan over a medium flame then add mushrooms and chopped bacon. Sauté until sizzling and add spinach.

5. Prepare Basic Egg Scramble, as directed on page 65. Pour egg mixture over bacon, mushrooms, and spinach. Stir until eggs are fully cooked, remove from heat, and serve.

Can't you just smell the sizzle? Tent walls are no match for the scent of bacon. Photo: Shaun Dunmall, Creative Commons on Flickr

Breakfast burritos are similar to huevos rancheros, but wrapped up in a flour tortilla instead of served on corn tortillas. Substitute hash browns for the beans and leave out the salsa for a different flavor combination. Adding bacon, ham, or sausage is never a bad idea.

Servings	4
PER SERVING	
Calories	571
Fat	28g
Protein	31g
Sodium	1357mg
Fiber	8g
Carbohydrates	49g
Sugar	5g
Vitamin A: 20% • Vitamin C: 3%	
Calcium: 40% • Iron: 30%	

INGREDIENTS

Basic Egg Scramble recipe, page 64
1 15-ounce can black beans or rehydrated
  dried beans
1 cup cheddar cheese, chopped or shredded
½ cup salsa
8 flour tortillas

METHOD

1. Drain beans and warm in frying pan over medium heat.

2. Prepare Basic Egg Scramble, as directed on page 65. Pour mixture over hot beans in pan.

3. Once eggs are cooked, cover with cheddar and remove from heat. Cover pan with a lid for 1 minute to let cheese melt.

4. While pan is covered, warm flour tortillas on the hot lid of the pan to make them more pliable and easier to wrap up.

5. Distribute salsa into four tortillas and top with cheesy egg-and-bean scramble.

6. Fold sides in and roll up burrito.

Omelet in a Bag

Serves: 1 | **Weight: 0.24 lbs.** | V

This is a truly fun and different way to make breakfast, with minimal cleanup. Depending on the size of your pot, you can boil 4 to 6 Omelets in a Bag at once. Everyone can customize their bags with their own blends of cheese, meats, and vegetables. Cleanup consists of washing your cheese grater!

Servings	1
PER SERVING	
Calories	**265**
Fat	19g
Protein	20g
Sodium	373mg
Fiber	0g
Carbohydrates	43g
Sugar	2g
Vitamin A: 15% • Vitamin C: 2%	
Calcium: 32% • Iron: 11%	

INGREDIENTS

2 quarts of water, or volume needed to cover bag(s) adequately, plus 6 tablespoons

4 tablespoons egg crystals

¼ cup cheddar cheese, shredded

2 tablespoons diced onion or 1 tablespoon onion powder

Optional: Bacon crumbles, diced salami, diced pepperoni, dried green pepper, garlic powder, dehydrated beef

METHOD

1. Boil water. While the water is heating up, measure egg crystals and 6 tablespoons of water into a quart-sized zippered storage bag. Massage bag to mix contents thoroughly.

2. Add cheese, onion, and any additional add-ins to egg mixture, mixing thoroughly. Roll bag to get most of the air out and seal completely.

3. Drop bag into the boiling water and boil for 13 minutes.

4. Fish the bag out of the water. The omelet should slip right out of the bag when opened.

5. Use some of the boiling water to rinse bag for reuse.

Backcountry Home Fries

Serves: 4	Weight: 0.4 lbs.	V	GF	NF		

Dehydrated hash browns are easy to find in most grocery stores and make for a very filling, lightweight addition to lots of recipes—or a great standalone treat. (You can also make your own in a dehydrator.) Try adding them to a soup, stir-fry, or scramble.

Servings	4
PER SERVING	
Calories	81
Fat	3g
Protein	1g
Sodium	15mg
Fiber	1g
Carbohydrates	12g
Sugar	1g
Vitamin A: 2% • Vitamin C: 11%	
Calcium: 2% • Iron: 3%	

INGREDIENTS

1 cup dehydrated hash browns
1 cup boiling water
1 tablespoon fresh butter
1 onion, chopped
1 clove garlic, minced

The closer a starch is to its natural state, the longer your energy will last. Photo: Laity Lodge Youth Camp, Creative Commons on Flickr

METHOD

1. Cover dehydrated hash browns with boiling water and stir.
2. Cover with a tight-fitting lid and let sit for 10 minutes or until potatoes are soft.
3. Drain excess water from potatoes.
4. While potatoes soak, heat butter in frying pan. Add onions and garlic.
5. Fry until onions are soft and translucent. Add drained potatoes and cook on medium flame until crispy and golden. Try not to stir frequently, as you want potatoes to get crispy.

Fried Bagels

| Serves: 1 | Weight: 0.25 lbs. | V | NF | |

Fried bagels make a delicious backcountry breakfast on the second day (first breakfast) of your trip, when no-preservative bagels will still be fresh and decidedly mold-free.

The magic here happens in the frying. Although the bagel you pull out of the bottom of your food bag may seem stale and unappetizing, frying it up in some butter will soften it and make it irresistible. Top with your favorite spread for a treat! Any vegetables you have on hand—including sun-dried tomatoes or bell pepper slices—make great additions to your bagel. Our favorite combination is cucumber and sliced red onions.

Servings	1
PER SERVING	
Calories	390
Fat	13g
Protein	11g
Sodium	562mg
Fiber	2g
Carbohydrates	56g
Sugar	0g
Vitamin A: 7% • Vitamin C: 0%	
Calcium: 2% • Iron: 21%	

INGREDIENTS

1 bagel
1 tablespoon fresh butter
Cream cheese to taste
Vegetables to taste

METHOD

1. Slice bagel and butter generously.
2. Cook butter-side down in a medium-hot frying pan for a minute or two. Once golden brown, flip over and cook for another minute or two to crisp up reverse side.
3. Remove and enjoy!

Peanut butter and jelly has long been relegated to lunch, but heating it up in a frying pan (with butter!) makes it a delicious, wholesome breakfast treat.

Servings	1
PER SERVING	
Calories	**458**
Fat	21g
Protein	12g
Sodium	443mg
Fiber	3g
Carbohydrates	59g
Sugar	18g
Vitamin A: 5% • Vitamin C: 4%	
Calcium: 7% • Iron: 12%	

INGREDIENTS

1 pita bread
2 teaspoons fresh butter
1½ tablespoons peanut butter
1½ tablespoons jelly or jam of choice

METHOD

1. Cut pita in half. Spread inner pockets of each half with peanut butter and jelly or jam.

2. Butter outsides of pita halves.

3. Fry over low flame (so it doesn't burn) until golden brown and gooey.

Tasha's Breakfast Couscous

Serves: 4 | **Weight: 0.6 lbs.** | V

INGREDIENTS

1 cup couscous, uncooked
⅛ teaspoon salt
1 cup powdered milk
2½ cups water, boiling
1 teaspoon cinnamon
½ cup raisins
½ cup slivered almonds
4 tablespoons maple syrup

Servings	4
PER SERVING	
Calories	**498**
Fat	15g
Protein	17g
Sodium	205mg
Fiber	5g
Carbohydrates	77g
Sugar	35g
Vitamin A: 6% • Vitamin C: 6%	
Calcium: 37% • Iron: 9%	

METHOD

1. Mix dry couscous, salt, and powdered milk together in a pot or heat-resistant bowl with tight-fitting lid.
2. Stir in boiling water until ingredients are incorporated then cover immediately.
3. Let stand 10 minutes without removing lid.
4. Remove lid and sprinkle with cinnamon.
5. Fluff with a fork and top with raisins, almonds, and maple syrup.

Want to dress up your couscous? Serve it in an orange. Photo: Tella Chen, Creative Commons on Flickr

Oatmeal

For oatmeal, we recommend using quick oats in the backcountry due to their quick cooking time and low fuel use. But you can always substitute rolled or steel cut oats; just increase your cooking time accordingly.

The combinations of oatmeal mix-ins are almost endless. Dried fruits, nuts, seeds, spices, and different sweeteners make each bowl unique and tasty.

Servings	1
PER SERVING	
Calories	153
Fat	3g
Protein	5g
Sodium	165mg
Fiber	4g
Carbohydrates	27g
Sugar	0g
Vitamin A: 0% • Vitamin C: 0%	
Calcium: 3% • Iron: 10%	

INGREDIENTS
1 cup water or milk
Dash of salt
½ cup quick oats

METHOD
1. Bring water or milk to a simmer and add salt.
2. Stir in oats.
3. Cook for 1 minute over medium to low flame. Stir frequently. Let cool for a couple minutes.

Dress up your oatmeal with any number of toppings, including:

Raisins	Flax seeds
Dried cranberries	Pumpkin seeds
Dried apples, chopped	Chia seeds
Dried cherries	Sesame seeds
Blueberries, fresh-picked or dried	Maple syrup
Dried apricots, chopped	Brown sugar
Dried strawberries	Honey
Dried mangos, chopped	Agave syrup
Slivered almonds	Chocolate chips
Pecans, chopped	Cinnamon
Walnuts, chopped	Allspice
Cashews, chopped	Nutmeg
Pistachios, shelled and chopped	Cardamom
Sunflower seeds	Ginger

Plain or garnished with goodies, whole-grain oatmeal is the breakfast of champs. Photo: OakleyOriginals, Creative Commons on Flickr

SWEET TREATS

Dottie's Downhome Coffee Cake

| AMC TRAIL-TESTED | Serves: 8 | Weight: 1.84 lbs. | V | |

Courtesy of Joe Roman, field coordinator for AMC's backcountry shelters

For decades, hut croo have awakened at dawn to bake this up for hungry hut guests and Appalachian Trail thru-hikers. Paired with copious amounts of butter, a hot cup of coffee, and some fresh-picked mountain blueberries, it's a perfect breakfast to eat as the sun rises. This recipe doubles the usual topping amount served in the huts. That's the way the Hipples made it back in the day. If you like a lighter topping, cut these amounts in half. But who likes light toppings? You can customize by adding blueberries, dried cherries, or ¼ teaspoon almond extract. You can also add ⅛ teaspoon nutmeg or slivered almonds. Or experiment with your own flavors!

Servings	8
PER SERVING	
Calories	**457**
Fat	13g
Protein	6g
Sodium	570mg
Fiber	2g
Carbohydrates	81g
Sugar	52g
Vitamin A: 9% • Vitamin C: 0%	
Calcium: 19% • Iron: 13%	

INGREDIENTS

Cake

4 tablespoons egg crystals
1 cup sugar
3 tablespoons powdered milk
½ cup butter powder or melted butter
2 cups flour
1 teaspoon salt
1 tablespoon plus 1 teaspoon baking powder
1¾ cups plus 2 tablespoons water

Topping

1 cup brown sugar
1 tablespoon plus 1 teaspoon cinnamon
¼ cup flour
¼ cup butter powder
2 tablespoons water

METHOD

1. Add water to cake ingredients stored in zippered bag and mix thoroughly. Snip a corner off the bag and squeeze batter into greased pan. Roll zippered storage bag like a toothpaste tube to get all batter and goodness out.

2. Add water to topping ingredients, mix thoroughly until crumbly.

3. Bake in fry-bake pan, reflector oven, or Dutch oven for 10 minutes then take out and sprinkle on topping. If you sprinkle from the start, the topping will sink to the bottom, and the sugars will cement the cake to the bottom of the pan.

4. Put topped cake back in heat and bake for another 30 minutes, removing when top is golden brown and a fork inserted into the middle comes out clean.

AMC hut croo begins breakfast prep early in the morning. Photo: Sue Rose

Sarah's Super-Sticky Caramel Rolls

| Makes: about 6 rolls | Weight: 1.23 lbs. | V | NF | |

You are in a warm sleeping bag, inside a tent, on an island, in the middle of a remote lake in northern New Hampshire. The sun rises, and birds start to chirp as mist rises off the lake. You smell coffee. And caramel. And warm yeasted dough baking near the fire. Someone (probably Sarah) woke up early to make Sarah's Super-Sticky Caramel Rolls. Life is good.

These are perfect for a rest day, when you have plenty of time and aren't in a rush to get out of camp. Just sit back and enjoy your breakfast masterpiece.

Servings	6
PER SERVING	
Calories	**536**
Fat	16g
Protein	15g
Sodium	337mg
Fiber	7g
Carbohydrates	87g
Sugar	33g
Vitamin A: 9% • Vitamin C: 0%	
Calcium: 6% • Iron: 19%	

INGREDIENTS

Dough
2 tablespoons egg crystals
2 tablespoons sugar
1 tablespoon powdered buttermilk or powdered milk
½ teaspoon salt
3 tablespoons butter powder
2 cups plus 2 tablespoons unbleached all-purpose white flour
2¼ teaspoons instant dry yeast
¾ cup water
½ cup flour or more, for dusting work surfaces

Caramel Glaze
3 tablespoons fresh butter
6 tablespoons brown sugar
2 tablespoons corn syrup (look for non-GMO and non-high-fructose varieties, or substitute with the replacement of your choice; e.g., cane syrup)
2 tablespoons powdered milk
⅛ teaspoon salt

Cinnamon Sugar Filling
6 tablespoons brown sugar
1 teaspoon cinnamon
¼ teaspoon cloves
⅛ teaspoon salt
1 tablespoon fresh butter, melted

METHOD

1. *At Home:* Separately pack dry ingredients for dough (except yeast), glaze, and filling in three quart-size bags, respectively. Pack yeast with dough but keep it in its packet or put it in its own smaller bag. Pack butter and corn syrup separately.

2. *On the Trail:* Flour a flexible cutting board or mat. In a bowl or pot, mix yeast with all dry dough ingredients. Add water and stir until evenly combined. If dough is still wet and sticky, add flour 1 tablespoon at a time.

3. Turn out dough onto a floured cutting mat, scraping as many bits and pieces of dough and flour as possible out of the bowl and onto mat. Knead for 5 minutes, adding flour as necessary to keep dough from sticking to mat and your hands.

4. Form dough into a smooth ball and place back in mixing bowl to rise. Put in a warm location: next to the stove or in the sun. If it's cold out and you can't find a warm spot in the sun, put dough in a 1-gallon zippered bag then put that inside a sleeping bag—and get in. With a person inside, the sleeping bag should be right about 98° F—the perfect temperature for yeast to activate and dough to rise. Let dough rise until it doubles in volume or 1 hour has passed, whichever comes first.

5. While dough is rising, mix glaze: Melt 3 tablespoons butter in Dutch oven, reflector oven, or fry-bake pan. Add corn syrup then empty dry glaze ingredients into butter. Stir for 5 minutes then remove from heat.

6. Pour half of glaze into a small bowl or cup, leaving the rest in the bottom of the baking dish and set aside.

7. When dough is done rising, turn it out onto a floured, flexible cutting board and knead for 1 minute. Gradually stretch dough into a roughly 8-by-11-inch rectangle, ¼- to ½-inch thick. Melt 1 tablespoon of butter and spread it around the rectangle, leaving a ¾-inch border around all edges. Sprinkle Cinnamon-Sugar Filling evenly over buttered portion of dough, pressing it in lightly with your hands.

8. Turn rectangle so long edge is nearest you then roll dough into a tight log. Firmly pinch seams to seal then roll the log, seam-side down.

9. Using a sharp serrated knife or dental floss, slice log into 6 to 8 wheels, which, when laid flat, will be rolls.

10. Place rolls evenly in Dutch oven, reflector oven, or fry-bake pan, right into the caramel sauce. Let rise for 20 to 30 minutes then bake for 25 to 30 minutes, checking often.

11. After rolls rise and turn golden brown, remove from heat, add remaining caramel glaze set aside earlier, and enjoy!

SECTION 5
COLD LUNCHES AND SNACKS ON THE GO

Setting up a stove at lunch means losing time and momentum in the backcountry. But if you've got lunch and snacks ready to go, you can spend that time enjoying a beautiful vista or covering new ground.

Mix and match items to create your own combinations. Make your lunches and snacks before you leave; stretch dinners into the next day; or pack simple, whole foods, smorgasbord-style. For the latter strategy, we bring a variety of crackers, cheese, peanut butter, fresh fruit, dried fruit, nuts, and pickles then enjoy whatever strikes our fancy. If you go this route, plan out your quantities ahead of time so you have enough to last the whole trip. We've listed approximate amounts per person. Keep in mind these quantities are for lunches only, not dinner and breakfast, as well.

- **Cheese:** 0.25 pound per person, per day
- **Peanut (or other nut) butter:** 3 tablespoons per person, per day
- **Salami:** 6 to 8 slices per person, per day
- **Tuna:** 5 ounces canned, per 2 people, per day
- **Crackers:** half a sleeve, per person, per day
- **Pita or pretzel chips:** 1 cup per person, per day
- **Bagels:** 1 per person, per day
- **Dried fruit:** ¼ cup per person, per day
- **Fresh fruit:** Harder fruits travel well; apples and oranges are best. Avoid soft fruits, such as peaches, bananas, berries, etc.
- **Nuts:** ¼ cup per person, per day

Photo: Ryan Kuonen, Creative Commons on Flickr

SMORGASBORD COMBOS

Cheddar and Slivered Garlic Lunch Combo

| Serves: 1 | Weight: 0.25 lbs. | V | NF | | |

INGREDIENTS
Hunk of cheddar cheese for slicing
1 clove of garlic, thinly sliced
6 crackers

METHOD
Something magical happens when you put a thin slice of garlic on a slice of aged cheddar. Add a cracker, chew, repeat.

Servings	1
PER SERVING	
Calories	132
Fat	10g
Protein	7g
Sodium	200mg
Fiber	0g
Carbohydrates	3g
Sugar	0g
Vitamin A: 6% • Vitamin C: 2%	
Calcium: 21% • Iron: 2%	

A no-fuss lunch lets you break anywhere that's LNT-friendly. Photo: Kevin Powlette/AMC Photo Contest

Sardines, Avocado, and Hardtack Lunch Combo

Serves: 1 | **Weight: 0.25 lbs.** | **DF**

This could be the most nutritious thing you eat on your trip. An old friend of ours is a backcountry ranger for the state of Maine. He patrols an area the size of Connecticut and eats this combo on the trail every day for lunch. It's full of the best kinds of fat, along with essential amino acids, and lots of umami. Hardtack is a simple bread or cracker made of only flour, water, and sometimes salt. It travels well and benefits from all kinds of toppings.

Servings	1
PER SERVING	
Calories	589
Fat	44g
Protein	28g
Sodium	608mg
Fiber	14g
Carbohydrates	26g
Sugar	26
Vitamin A: 8% • Vitamin C: 34%	
Calcium: 39% • Iron: 24%	

INGREDIENTS

1 can of sardines
1 avocado, sliced thin
5 crackers

METHOD

Eat as you will.

FRUIT LEATHERS

Basic Fruit Leather Method

Makes: 6 to 12 rolls

INGREDIENTS
4 cups chopped fruit
¾ cup sugar
1 to 2 tablespoons lemon juice, to taste

METHOD
1. Preheat oven to 200° F. Line an 18-by-26-inch rimmed cookie sheet with aluminum foil or a nonstick silicone baking mat.
2. Put fruit, sugar, and lemon juice in a blender. Purée until smooth.
3. Transfer mixture to saucepan. Cook over medium heat for 30 to 40 minutes, stirring frequently so mixture doesn't stick or burn.
4. Once mixture has thickened considerably, pour into prepared pan, spreading evenly.
5. Bake until most of the liquid has evaporated and mixture is barely tacky and leathery. This will take about 3 hours, possibly longer.
6. Remove from oven and let cool completely.
7. Peel fruit leather from pan. Work slowly from one corner, trying to get it all in one piece.
8. If fruit is still wet on the underside, turn it wet-side up and put pan back in the oven for 15 to 20 minutes.
9. Once peeled, lay fruit leather on the counter, smooth-side up, and cover it with a layer of waxed paper. Working from the short end, roll entire sheet lengthwise into a big roll.
10. Using a serrated knife, cut roll into 1- or 2-inch sections.
11. Store in zippered storage bag for up to a week or keep in freezer up to 6 months.

Sweet and Spicy Mango Fruit Leather

Makes: 6 to 12 rolls | **Weight: 0.31 lbs.** | V | V+ | DF | GF |

INGREDIENTS

4 cups chopped fresh mango
¾ cup sugar
2 tablespoons lemon juice
⅛ teaspoon salt
¼ teaspoon cayenne pepper, or to taste

METHOD

Prepare as directed in Basic Fruit Leather Method,
page 86, adding salt and cayenne to blender along with
other ingredients.

Servings	6
PER SERVING	
Calories	170
Fat	0g
Protein	1g
Sodium	53mg
Fiber	2g
Carbohydrates	44g
Sugar	42g
Vitamin A: 17% • Vitamin C: 53%	
Calcium: 1% • Iron: 1%	

With homemade fruit leather, the flavor options are endless. Photo: Bamonahan, Creative Commons on Flickr

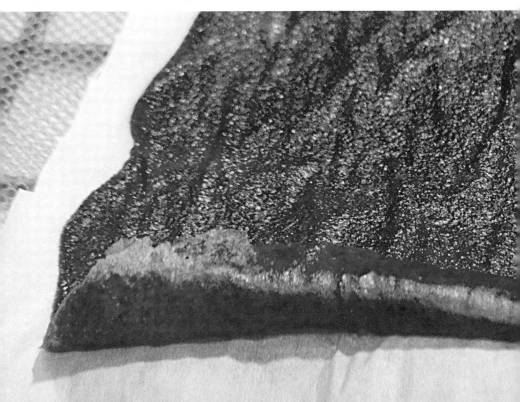

Strawberry Fruit Leather

Makes: 6 to 12 rolls | **Weight: 0.31 lbs.** | V V+ DF GF

INGREDIENTS
4 cups strawberries, chopped
¾ cup sugar
1 tablespoon lemon juice

METHOD
Prepare as directed in Basic Fruit Leather Method, page 86.

Servings	6
PER SERVING	
Calories	129
Fat	0g
Protein	1g
Sodium	52mg
Fiber	2g
Carbohydrates	33g
Sugar	30g
Vitamin A: 0% • Vitamin C: 95%	
Calcium: 2% • Iron: 2%	

Mixed Berry Fruit Leather

Makes: 6 to 12 rolls | **Weight: 0.31 lbs.** | V V+ DF GF

INGREDIENTS
2 cups blueberries, chopped
1 cup strawberries, chopped
1 cup raspberries, chopped
¾ cup sugar
1 teaspoon lemon juice

METHOD
Prepare as directed in Basic Fruit Leather Method, page 86.

Servings	6
PER SERVING	
Calories	144
Fat	0g
Protein	1g
Sodium	1mg
Fiber	3g
Carbohydrates	37g
Sugar	32g
Vitamin A: 1% • Vitamin C: 41%	
Calcium: 1% • Iron: 2%	

JERKIES

Basic Beef Jerky Method

Serves: 8–16

INGREDIENTS
1 pound beef, ideally flank or skirt steak, although ground beef works
Marinade ingredients of your choosing (see variations that follow)

METHOD
1. Trim any large pieces of fat from meat. Place meat in a zippered storage bag and put in freezer for 1 hour until it becomes stiff and easy to slice thinly.
2. Remove beef from bag and slice, with the grain, into long strips about ¼-inch thick. Place strips back in bag.
3. In a medium bowl, whisk marinade ingredients. Pour on top of steak and reseal bag.
4. Refrigerate marinating steak for 6 to 12 hours.
5. Preheat oven to lowest temperature possible, but no lower than 170° F and ideally no higher than 200° F. If you have a convection oven, turn the convection fan on.
6. Remove beef strips from marinade and pat dry with a paper towel. Lay strips out, being careful not to overlap, on a wire cooling rack placed on top of a rimmed baking sheet.
7. Bake for 3 to 4 hours or until beef seems adequately dried and no redness remains.
8. Let cool and cut into strips with kitchen scissors.
9. Store in zippered storage bag for up to 2 weeks or keep in freezer for 3 to 6 months.

Teriyaki Beef Jerky

Serves: 8	Weight: 0.25 lbs.	DF	GF

INGREDIENTS

1 pound London broil
2 tablespoons brown sugar
¼ cup sugar
1½ teaspoons kosher salt
2 teaspoons minced garlic
1 teaspoon minced ginger
¼ teaspoon coarsely ground black pepper
2 tablespoons rice wine
1 cup pineapple juice
½ cup water
1 tablespoon honey
½ cup soy sauce or tamari

Servings	8
PER SERVING	
Calories	**153**
Fat	2g
Protein	14g
Sodium	1398mg
Fiber	0g
Carbohydrates	18g
Sugar	15g
Vitamin A: 0% • Vitamin C: 6%	
Calcium: 2% • Iron: 9%	

METHOD

Prepare as directed in Basic Beef Jerky Method, page 89.

Honey Barbecue Beef Jerky

Serves: 8	Weight: 0.25 lbs.	GF

INGREDIENTS

1 pound flank steak or London broil
¾ cup honey
½ cup ketchup
¼ cup fresh butter
1 tablespoon cider vinegar
2 teaspoons Dijon mustard
3 tablespoons brown sugar
1 tablespoon soy sauce or tamari
1 teaspoon minced garlic
1½ teaspoon chili powder

Servings	8
PER SERVING	
Calories	**273**
Fat	10g
Protein	13g
Sodium	333mg
Fiber	0g
Carbohydrates	37g
Sugar	35g
Vitamin A: 9% • Vitamin C: 5%	
Calcium: 3% • Iron: 7%	

METHOD

Prepare as directed in Basic Beef Jerky Method, page 89.

It's even more delicious when you make it yourself. Photo: Ryan.Dowd, Creative Commons on Flickr

Peppered Beef Jerky

| Serves: 16 | Weight: 0.5 lbs. | DF | NF | 🏠 |

INGREDIENTS

2 pounds flank steak

⅔ cup soy sauce or tamari

¾ cup Worcestershire sauce

2 tablespoons honey

2 tablespoons coarsely ground black pepper

2 teaspoons onion powder

1 teaspoon red pepper flakes

Servings	16
PER SERVING	
Calories	114
Fat	4g
Protein	13g
Sodium	756ng
Fiber	0g
Carbohydrates	6g
Sugar	4g
Vitamin A: 1% • Vitamin C: 3%	
Calcium: 3% • Iron: 11%	

METHOD

Prepare as directed in Basic Beef Jerky Method, page 89.

Malaysian Pork Jerky (Bak Kwa)

Serves: 8 | **Weight: 0.25 lbs.** | GF | NF |

INGREDIENTS

1 pound ground pork
1 tablespoon rice wine
2 teaspoons soy sauce or tamari
2 teaspoons fish sauce
2 teaspoons sesame oil
⅓ cup sugar
¼ teaspoon pepper
½ teaspoon five-spice powder

Servings	8
PER SERVING	
Calories	194
Fat	13g
Protein	10g
Sodium	222mg
Fiber	0g
Carbohydrates	9g
Sugar	8g
Vitamin A: 0% • Vitamin C: 1%	
Calcium: 9% • Iron: 3%	

METHOD

1. Place all ingredients in a bowl. Stir well to combine. Cover the bowl and place in the refrigerator for 4 to 8 hours.
2. Preheat the oven to 250° F.
3. Cut parchment paper to fit in the bottom of 3 rimmed baking sheets. (Alternatively, this method could be followed with one baking sheet at a time; in that case, keep remaining meat in refrigerator until ready for use.)
4. Spread ⅓ of the meat onto each of the parchment papers and, using an offset spatula, spread evenly over the paper.
5. Cover the meat with plastic wrap and use a rolling pin to further even out the pork.
6. Remove the plastic wrap and put each sheet of meat onto a baking sheet in the oven. Bake for 20 minutes.
7. Remove from the oven and use a paper towel to blot any liquid off the jerky. Let cool until can be handled.
8. Turn the oven up to 425° F.
9. Cut each sheet into 6 or 12 pieces (depending on the size that you like). Return the pieces to the parchment paper on the baking sheets.
10. Continue baking for about 5 minutes, or until it browns but isn't burned.
11. Flip the strips over and cook for another 5 minutes on the second side. Monitor oven carefully to keep strips from burning.
12. Remove pans from oven. Cool strips thoroughly on a wire rack before storing in a zippered storage bag for up to 3 weeks or up to 6 months in a freezer.

NUTS AND NUT BUTTERS

Sweet and Spicy Rosemary Cashews

Makes: 2 cups **Weight: 0.56 lbs.** V GF

INGREDIENTS

2 cups cashews
1½ tablespoons fresh butter
2 teaspoons brown sugar
¼ teaspoon cayenne pepper
2 tablespoons fresh rosemary, chopped
1 teaspoon sea salt

Servings	4
PER SERVING	
Calories	326
Fat	30g
Protein	10g
Sodium	1620mg
Fiber	1g
Carbohydrates	26g
Sugar	4g
Vitamin A: 4% • Vitamin C: 1%	
Calcium: 3% • Iron: 23%	

METHOD

1. Preheat oven to 375° F. Line a rimmed baking sheet with parchment paper.

2. Spread cashews in one layer on baking sheet. Bake for 8 to 12 minutes. Shake tray often throughout baking so nuts don't burn. While cashews roast, prepare remaining ingredients.

3. Melt butter in a large bowl and allow to cool slightly. Add brown sugar, cayenne, rosemary, and salt to warm butter and stir to combine until sugar is slightly dissolved.

4. Take cashews out of the oven and carefully stir hot nuts into spice mixture with a large spoon to coat. Cool cashews in a single layer on parchment baking sheet. Keep in an airtight container for up to 2 weeks.

Chipotle Honey Roasted Nuts are jam-packed with energy to keep you hiking. Photo: Whitney, Creative Commons on Flickr

Chipotle Honey Roasted Peanuts

Makes: 3 cups | **Weight: 1.14 lbs.** | V | GF

INGREDIENTS

½ cup sugar
½ teaspoon chipotle chili powder
1 teaspoon chili powder
¼ teaspoon garlic powder
2 tablespoons fresh butter
2 tablespoons honey
1 teaspoon salt
3 cups peanuts

Servings	6
PER SERVING	
Calories	283
Fat	16g
Protein	9g
Sodium	149mg
Fiber	5g
Carbohydrates	31g
Sugar	24g
Vitamin A: 0% • Vitamin C: 0%	
Calcium: 3% • Iron: 5%	

METHOD

1. Preheat oven to 300° F.

2. In a small bowl, stir together sugar and spices then set aside.

3. In a saucepan, melt butter, honey, and salt together.

4. Stir in peanuts and coat thoroughly.

5. Dump hot, gooey nuts out onto a rimmed cookie sheet and bake for 30 minutes, or until nuts are golden brown.

6. Remove peanuts from the oven. While nuts are still hot, scrape them into a heat-proof bowl, sprinkle sugar-and-spice mixture over them, and toss to coat.

7. Stir periodically until nuts are cool. Keep in an airtight container for up to 2 weeks.

Curried Almonds

Makes: 3½ cups | Weight: 1.09 lbs. | V | V+ | DF | GF |

INGREDIENTS

2 tablespoons coconut oil

1 tablespoon maple syrup

3 tablespoons sugar

1 tablespoon curry powder

⅛ teaspoon cayenne pepper

1½ teaspoons salt

3 cups almonds

½ cup shredded coconut (check labels and choose an unsweetened, single-ingredient version)

1 tablespoon white sesame seeds

Servings	7
PER SERVING	
Calories	**412**
Fat	35g
Protein	10g
Sodium	512mg
Fiber	8g
Carbohydrates	21g
Sugar	10g
Vitamin A: 0% • Vitamin C: 1%	
Calcium: 13% • Iron: 14%	

METHOD

1. Preheat oven to 300° F.

2. Combine coconut oil, syrup, sugar, and spices in a medium-sized, microwave-safe bowl and microwave for 1 minute to melt coconut oil.

3. Stir until smooth. Add remaining ingredients and toss to coat evenly.

4. Dump hot, gooey nuts out onto a rimmed cookie sheet and bake for 30 minutes, or until nuts are golden brown.

5. Remove from oven and stir periodically until nuts are cool. Keep in an airtight container for up to 2 weeks.

Curried almonds satisfy sweet and spicy cravings.
Photo: Fox-and-Fern, Creative Commons on Flickr

Cinnamon-Spiced Pecans

Makes: 4 cups | **Weight: 1.23 lbs.** | V | DF | GF | NF |

INGREDIENTS

½ cup sugar
3 teaspoons ground cinnamon
½ teaspoon salt
1 egg white
4 cups pecans, halved

Servings	8
PER SERVING	
Calories	429
Fat	40g
Protein	5g
Sodium	154mg
Fiber	6g
Carbohydrates	21g
Sugar	15g
Vitamin A: 1% • Vitamin C: 1%	
Calcium: 5% • Iron: 8%	

METHOD

1. Preheat oven to 300° F.

2. Combine sugar, salt, and cinnamon in a bowl and set aside.

3. Whisk egg white in large bowl until smooth.

4. Toss in pecans and coat thoroughly.

5. Sprinkle pecans with sugar mixture and toss to coat. Spread on a rimmed baking sheet. Bake for 30 minutes or until nuts are golden brown.

6. Remove pecans from the oven and stir periodically until nuts are cool. Keep in an airtight container for up to 2 weeks.

Pecans are a good source of dietary fiber, fat, protein, iron, and B vitamins. Photo: Jennifer Wehunt

Classic Good Old Raisins and Peanuts (GORP)

Makes: 4 cups | **Weight: 0.33 lbs. per cup** | V | GF

INGREDIENTS
2 cups dry-roasted, salted peanuts
1 cup raisins
1 cup semisweet chocolate chips

METHOD
Mix ingredients in a large bowl until thoroughly distributed. Store in an airtight container away from direct heat.

Servings	8
PER SERVING	
Calories	390
Fat	24g
Protein	11g
Sodium	25mg
Fiber	5g
Carbohydrates	39g
Sugar	29g
Vitamin A: 1% • Vitamin C: 1%	
Calcium: 7% • Iron: 13%	

Tropical Trail Mix

Makes: 3 cups | **Weight: 0.33 lbs. per cup** | V

INGREDIENTS
¼ cup shredded coconut (check labels and choose an
  unsweetened, single-ingredient version)
¾ cup slivered almonds
½ cup raw pepitas (pumpkin seeds)
¾ cup cashews
½ cup dried pineapple
¼ cup dried mango or papaya, chopped
2 tablespoons candied ginger, finely chopped

Servings	6
PER SERVING	
Calories	150
Fat	10g
Protein	4g
Sodium	141mg
Fiber	3g
Carbohydrates	14g
Sugar	7g
Vitamin A: 1% • Vitamin C: 14%	
Calcium: 4% • Iron: 5%	

METHOD
Mix ingredients in a large bowl until thoroughly distributed. Store in an airtight container away from direct heat.

ABOVE: Get creative when assembling your own trail mix: Sub in cranberries for cherries or sunflower seeds for pistachios. Photo: Cary Bass-Deschenes, Creative Commons on Flickr

RIGHT: Making your own nut butters means you know exactly what's in them. Photo: Justin Grimes, Creative Commons on Flickr

Fruits and Nuts Trail Mix

Makes: 4 cups | **Weight: 1.6 lbs.** | V V+ DF GF

INGREDIENTS

¾ cup pistachio nuts, shelled
¾ cup cashews, halved
1 cup honey-roasted peanuts
½ cup dried cherries, chopped
1 cup semisweet chocolate chips

METHOD

Mix ingredients in a large bowl until thoroughly distributed. Store in an airtight container away from direct heat.

Servings	8
PER SERVING	
Calories	**451**
Fat	14g
Protein	14g
Sodium	232mg
Fiber	6g
Carbohydrates	30g
Sugar	16g
Vitamin A: 1% • Vitamin C: 2%	
Calcium: 4% • Iron: 18%	

Cashew Butter

We could eat this on everything: pancakes, tortillas, bagels, crackers, and even carrot sticks. It's even delicious on its own, by the spoonful. You can substitute roasted almonds, pecans, pistachios, or sunflower seeds for different and equally delicious flavors.

Servings	16
PER SERVING	
Calories	116
Fat	12g
Protein	1g
Sodium	222mg
Fiber	0g
Carbohydrates	3g
Sugar	2g
Vitamin A: 0% • Vitamin C: 0%	
Calcium: 0% • Iron: 1%	

INGREDIENTS

2 cups cashews
¾ cup coconut oil
2 tablespoons honey
1½ teaspoons salt
½ teaspoon vanilla extract

METHOD

1. Place nuts and salt in food processor then blend until smooth.

2. Add honey and coconut oil then process again until buttery.

3. Store in an airtight container for 3 to 4 weeks.

Chocolate Hazelnut Heaven

Makes: 2 cups | **Weight: 1.32 lbs.** | V

Possibly the best thing you will bring on your trip, this is a recipe you will find yourself making all the time—at home or for the wilderness. It's just delicious, period. Good luck rationing this to last longer than a couple of days. We prefer the homemade variety because it has a little more texture than the store-bought stuff. If you prefer it super smooth, use a Vitamix blender rather than a food processor.

Servings	16
PER SERVING	
Calories	154
Fat	11g
Protein	3g
Sodium	37mg
Fiber	2g
Carbohydrates	15g
Sugar	12g
Vitamin A: 0% • Vitamin C: 2%	
Calcium: 2% • Iron: 5%	

INGREDIENTS

2 cups hazelnuts, shelled
1½ cups powdered sugar
⅓ cup cocoa powder
2 tablespoons hazelnut oil or vegetable oil
1½ teaspoons vanilla
¼ teaspoon salt

METHOD

1. Preheat oven to 350° F.
2. Roast hazelnuts on a baking sheet for 15 to 20 minutes, or until the nuts turn golden brown.
3. Remove nuts and place them in a medium-sized bowl. Invert another, similarly sized bowl on top of nuts and, holding both bowls together in your hands, shake vigorously to remove papery skins from nuts. It isn't critical to remove *all* skins, but they give the spread a bitterness if most aren't removed.
4. Put nuts and remaining ingredients into a food processor and let it run for several minutes, stopping to scrape bowl several times throughout, until it reaches your desired consistency.
5. Pour spread into any airtight container. No need to refrigerate.

VEGGIE NIBBLES AND SPREADS

Ants on a Log

Serves: 1 | Weight: 0.4 lbs. | V V+ DF GF

Yes, the classic toddler snack is also a great backcountry lunch. The celery won't keep long in the backcountry, so eat it during the first day or two of your trip.

INGREDIENTS
4 stalks celery
¼ cup peanut butter
¼ cup raisins

METHOD
Spread the peanut butter in the cavity of the celery, top with a smattering of raisins, and enjoy!

Servings	1
PER SERVING	
Calories	311
Fat	17g
Protein	10g
Sodium	216mg
Fiber	5g
Carbohydrates	38g
Sugar	26g
Vitamin A: 7% • Vitamin C: 6%	
Calcium: 7% • Iron: 8%	

When you need a treat, substitute chocolate ants for raisins. Photo: Essie, Creative Commons on Flickr

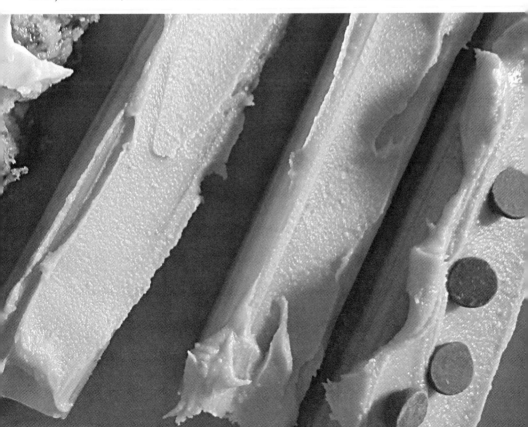

Banana Boat

Bananas don't do well in the backcountry, as they get mushed almost the instant you put them in your pack. But if you eat them the first day, this is a delicious treat—and just a fun way to eat a banana.

Servings	1
PER SERVING	
Calories	294
Fat	17g
Protein	9g
Sodium	149mg
Fiber	5g
Carbohydrates	33g
Sugar	17g
Vitamin A: 2% • Vitamin C: 17%	
Calcium: 20% • Iron: 5%	

INGREDIENTS

1 banana
2 tablespoons peanut butter

METHOD

1. Instead of peeling the banana as usual, take off one strip of banana peel and leave the rest intact on the banana.
2. Slice the banana in the peel. Spread peanut butter across the exposed top.
3. Spoon out of the peel, one slice at a time.

Peanut Butter-Filled Dates

Serves: 4 | Weight: 1.05 lbs. |

INGREDIENTS

16 pitted dates

½ cup peanut butter

Optional toppings: chocolate chips, coconut, sea salt, chopped nuts

METHOD

Split open each date and spread with a spoonful of peanut butter. Close dates around peanut butter and store in an airtight container.

Servings	4
PER SERVING	
Calories	283
Fat	16g
Protein	9g
Sodium	149mg
Fiber	5g
Carbohydrates	31g
Sugar	24g
Vitamin A: 0% • Vitamin C: 0%	
Calcium: 3% • Iron: 5%	

Already a source of potassium, dates stuffed with peanut butter provide extra protein. Photo: Denise Krebs, Creative Commons on Flickr

Buffalo Cauliflower "Popcorn"

Makes: 2 cups **Weight: 0.38 lbs.** V V+ DF GF NF

INGREDIENTS

½ cup dates
¼ cup water
2 tablespoons sun-dried tomatoes
1 tablespoon nutritional yeast
1 tablespoon tahini
2 teaspoons cider vinegar
½ teaspoon cayenne pepper
1 teaspoon garlic powder
1 teaspoon onion powder
⅛ teaspoon turmeric
1 head cauliflower, chopped into very small florets
Sea salt to taste

Servings	4
PER SERVING	
Calories	138
Fat	3g
Protein	6g
Sodium	247mg
Fiber	6g
Carbohydrates	27g
Sugar	18g
Vitamin A: 2% • Vitamin C: 117%	
Calcium: 7% • Iron: 9%	

METHOD

1. Put all ingredients except cauliflower in food processor and blend until a smooth paste forms.

2. In a large bowl, stir cauliflower florets and paste until cauliflower is thoroughly coated.

3. *In a dehydrator:* Spread cauliflower onto dehydrator trays and sprinkle with sea salt. Dehydrate on low for around 12 hours, or until cauliflower has reached desired level of crunch.

4. *Without a dehydrator:* Put cauliflower on a rimmed baking sheet and set your oven on its lowest setting. Bake for several hours, until cauliflower reaches desired level of crunch. An oven set to 170° F will dry cauliflower in about 4 hours.

Hummus

Hummus and other spreads keep best in the backcountry when dehydrated. But rehydrating them requires hot water, and no one wants hot hummus! To get around this conundrum, simply heat a little extra water during breakfast and rehydrate the mix in one of your sealable containers. By the time you get to your lunch destination, it will have rehydrated and cooled off.

Servings	8
PER SERVING	
Calories	288
Fat	14g
Protein	11g
Sodium	243mg
Fiber	9g
Carbohydrates	32g
Sugar	6g
Vitamin A: 1% • Vitamin C: 6%	
Calcium: 9% • Iron: 21%	

INGREDIENTS

2 15-ounce cans chickpeas, drained and rinsed
1 clove garlic
¾ teaspoons salt
⅛ teaspoon cayenne pepper
3 tablespoons lemon juice
¼ cup tahini
¼ cup olive oil
¼ cup water

METHOD

1. Place all ingredients in food processor. Process until it reaches a smooth texture.

2. *If carrying fresh:* Refrigerate in an airtight container and use on the first day of your trip.

3. *If dehydrating:* Spread thinly on dehydrating mats and dry at 135° F for 6 to 8 hours. After about 5 hours, peel hummus off mats and let it sit directly on dehydrating trays, so both sides are exposed to air. Rehydrate with a 1:1 ratio of water a few hours before your meal.

Edamame Herb Hummus

| Makes: 1½ cups | Weight: 0.51 lbs. fresh, 0.12 lbs. dehydrated |

INGREDIENTS

1 cup cooked edamame, shelled
¼ cup tahini
2 tablespoons lemon juice
1 teaspoon garlic powder
2 tablespoons chopped fresh basil and/or parsley
3 tablespoons olive oil
½ teaspoon salt

METHOD

Prepare as directed in Hummus method, page 105.

Servings	6
PER SERVING	
Calories	163
Fat	14g
Protein	6g
Sodium	213mg
Fiber	2g
Carbohydrates	6g
Sugar	0g
Vitamin A: 2% • Vitamin C: 11%	
Calcium: 9% • Iron: 10%	

Yum, hummus. Add edamame for flavor or get creative with herbs. Photo: Jennifer Wehunt

INGREDIENTS

1 15-ounce can black beans, drained and rinsed

2 tablespoons salsa

1 tablespoon water

2 cloves garlic, roughly chopped

2 teaspoons lime juice

¼ teaspoon cumin

½ teaspoon salt

⅛ teaspoon cayenne pepper

2 green onions, chopped

Servings	6
PER SERVING	
Calories	65
Fat	1g
Protein	4g
Sodium	437mg
Fiber	4g
Carbohydrates	12g
Sugar	2g
Vitamin A: 4% • Vitamin C: 5%	
Calcium: 3% • Iron: 5%	

METHOD

Prepare as directed in Hummus method, page 105.

INGREDIENTS

1 15-ounce can cannellini beans, drained and rinsed

2 cloves garlic

2 tablespoons lemon juice

⅓ cup olive oil

¼ cup fresh parsley

⅛ teaspoon salt

⅛ teaspoon pepper

Servings	7
PER SERVING	
Calories	145
Fat	10g
Protein	4g
Sodium	203mg
Fiber	3g
Carbohydrates	10g
Sugar	1g
Vitamin A: 4% • Vitamin C: 7%	
Calcium: 1% • Iron: 1%	

METHOD

Prepare as directed in Hummus method, page 105.

GRANOLA BARS

Double Chocolate Granola Bars

Makes: 12 bars | **Weight: 1.85 lbs.** | V | V+ | DF | GF

INGREDIENTS

1½ cups rolled oats
1 cup slivered almonds
2 cups pitted dates
¾ cup cocoa powder
¼ cup maple syrup
¼ cup almond butter
½ cup semisweet chocolate chips

Servings	12
PER SERVING	
Calories	341
Fat	26g
Protein	8g
Sodium	4mg
Fiber	8g
Carbohydrates	48g
Sugar	29g
Vitamin A: 0% • Vitamin C: 0%	
Calcium: 6% • Iron: 27%	

METHOD

1. Line a 9-by-13-inch pan with parchment paper.
2. Spread oats and almonds evenly on a rimmed baking sheet and bake at 350° F for 10 to 15 minutes, until mix begins to brown.
3. Soak dates in warm water for 10 minutes then drain.
4. Process dates in a food processor for about a minute, or until they form a doughlike ball.
5. Add cocoa powder to dates and continue to process until combined.
6. Transfer mixture to a large bowl and add in oats and almonds. This will be too hard to stir with a spoon, so you will need to knead the mix with your hands.
7. Heat maple syrup and almond butter together for 1 minute in a microwave-safe bowl or on the stovetop, stirring regularly until smooth.
8. Pour liquid over date mixture and combine thoroughly with your hands.
9. Press mix into prepared pan and refrigerate for 1 hour to set up.
10. Remove from pan and cut into 12 bars.
11. Wrap each bar individually with plastic wrap for easy access on the trail.

Cherry Choco-Nut Granola Bars

Makes: 12 bars | **Weight: 1.2 lbs.** | V | V+ | DF | GF |

Pairing chocolate and cherries is like pairing peanut butter and jelly. Or mozzarella and tomatoes. The combination just works.

Servings	12
PER SERVING	
Calories	196
Fat	18g
Protein	5g
Sodium	47mg
Fiber	2g
Carbohydrates	18g
Sugar	8g
Vitamin A: 1% • Vitamin C: 2%	
Calcium: 3% • Iron: 14%	

INGREDIENTS

1 cup cashews, chopped
½ cup slivered almonds
½ cup dried cherries, chopped
½ cup puffed rice cereal
¼ cup pumpkin seeds
½ cup semisweet chocolate chips
⅛ teaspoon sea salt
1 tablespoon flax seeds
¼ cup corn syrup (look for non-GMO and non-high-fructose varieties, or substitute with the replacement of your choice; e.g., cane syrup)
1 tablespoon peanut butter

METHOD

1. Preheat oven to 325° F. Line 8-by-8-inch baking pan with parchment paper.
2. Mix all dry ingredients together in a medium-sized bowl.
3. In a small bowl, combine the corn syrup and peanut butter. Stir into nut mixture until thoroughly combined.
4. Using an extra sheet of parchment paper, press sticky mix into the pan.
5. Bake for 15 minutes. Allow to cool completely in pan.
6. Remove from pan and cut into 12 bars.
7. Wrap each bar individually with plastic wrap for easy access on the trail.

Chocolate Peanut Butter Granola Bars

INGREDIENTS

⅔ cup corn syrup (look for non-GMO and non-high-fructose varieties, or substitute with the replacement of your choice; e.g., cane syrup)

½ cup peanut butter

⅓ cup brown sugar

2 teaspoons vanilla

¼ cup cocoa powder

1 teaspoon salt

2 cups quick oats

2 cups puffed rice cereal

1 cup semisweet chocolate chips, divided

Servings	12
PER SERVING	
Calories	310
Fat	12g
Protein	6g
Sodium	297mg
Fiber	4g
Carbohydrates	49g
Sugar	23g
Vitamin A: 2% • Vitamin C: 5%	
Calcium: 3% • Iron: 17%	

METHOD

1. Line an 8-by-8-inch pan with parchment paper and spray with a flavor-neutral greasing agent (such as butter).

2. In a microwave-safe bowl, combine corn syrup, peanut butter, and brown sugar. Microwave for 1 minute and stir until smooth.

3. Add vanilla, cocoa, salt, and whisk again until smooth.

4. Stir in oats, rice cereal, and ¾ cup chocolate chips until thoroughly combined.

5. Using an extra sheet of parchment paper, press mix into pan.

6. Evenly sprinkle with last ¼ cup of chocolate chips, pressing lightly so chips adhere to mixture.

7. Allow to cool completely in pan.

8. Cut into 12 bars. Wrap each bar individually with plastic wrap for easy access on the trail.

Chocolate and peanut butter deliver protein and a burst of energy. Photo: Abigail Coyle

Blueberry Granola Bars with Vanilla Icing

Makes: 12 bars | **Weight: 1.5 lbs.** | V | GF

INGREDIENTS

Bars

1½ cup puffed rice cereal

2 cups rolled oats

¼ cup chopped, roasted almonds

¼ cup shredded coconut (check labels and choose an unsweetened, single-ingredient version)

2 tablespoons chia seeds

¼ teaspoon salt

¾ cup dried blueberries

½ cup almond butter

½ cup honey

2 teaspoons vanilla

Vanilla Icing

1 tablespoon water

2 teaspoons vanilla extract

½ teaspoon gelatin

¼ cup plain yogurt

⅛ teaspoon salt

1 tablespoon honey

2 cups powdered sugar

Servings	12
PER SERVING	
Calories	291
Fat	9g
Protein	6g
Sodium	155mg
Fiber	3g
Carbohydrates	50g
Sugar	36g
Vitamin A: 2% • Vitamin C: 6%	
Calcium: 5% • Iron: 13%	

METHOD

1. Line a 9-by-13-inch baking pan with wax paper.

2. In a large bowl, combine all dry ingredients, including dried blueberries.

3. In a smaller, microwave-safe bowl, combine almond butter, honey, and vanilla. Microwave for about 30 seconds, or until warm enough to stir into a smooth liquid.

4. Pour liquid over dry ingredients and mix well.

5. Dump sticky mixture into prepared pan and press into all corners with the heel of your hand or the back of a spatula.

6. Place pan in freezer for 30 minutes to set.

7. While pan is chilling, prepare icing. In a small bowl, combine water, vanilla, and gelatin.

8. In a larger, microwave-safe bowl, combine yogurt, salt, and honey. Microwave until warm and very loose. Whisk well.

9. Pour gelatin mixture into the yogurt mixture and mix thoroughly. Stir until all gelatin is dissolved. Add powdered sugar.
10. Take the pan out of the freezer and lift the loaf from the pan using the edge of the wax paper. Cut into bars.
11. Line a baking sheet with another sheet of wax paper.
12. Take each bar and dip half into icing. Hold the bar over the bowl of icing and let the extra drip into the bowl. Place bars icing-side up on lined pan. Repeat with each bar until they're all iced.
13. Let bars dry overnight so icing hardens. Wrap each bar individually with plastic wrap for easy access on the trail.

To cut down on sugar, skip the icing dip. Photo: JeffreyW, Creative Commons on Flickr

Ski Bars

These are a perfect midday pick-me-up while skiing or hiking in cooler weather. The bars are sweet and delicious but can be on the soft side; make sure to wrap them well so they don't make a mess in your pack. Keep any extras in the freezer for up to 6 months; frozen bars kept in a pack should thaw enough to eat in a few hours.

Servings	24
PER SERVING	
Calories	269
Fat	14g
Protein	8g
Sodium	102mg
Fiber	3g
Carbohydrates	32g
Sugar	24g
Vitamin A: 2% • Vitamin C: 0%	
Calcium: 2% • Iron: 8%	

INGREDIENTS

2 cups creamy peanut butter
1 cup honey
4 cups rolled oats
½ cup oat bran
¼ cup shredded coconut (check labels and choose an unsweetened, single-ingredient version)
¼ cup water
¼ cup slivered almonds
¼ cup chopped walnuts
½ cup dried fruit, chopped
½ cup semisweet chocolate chips

METHOD

1. Line a 9-by-11-inch pan with parchment paper.
2. Mix all ingredients together in large bowl.
3. Press into lined pan.
4. Place pan in refrigerator for one hour, until mixture sets and chills completely.
5. Cut into 12 bars. Wrap each bar individually with plastic wrap for easy access on the trail.

SECTION 6
HOT DINNERS AT CAMP

And now we come to the true heart of this book: hot dishes of all sizes you can prepare on the trail. A hot meal never tastes better than it does outdoors, especially after a long and challenging day. When you're sitting back to enjoy a delicious, savory dinner, you'll be thankful for all of your planning and prep work before leaving home.

Most meals in this section require some prep at home and some on the trail, even if the former is just repackaging or the latter is just heating up. But we've kept the work you do on the trail as simple as possible. After a long day in the backcountry, you'll want food, hot and fast, and these recipes should hit the spot.

You'll notice some recipes in this chapter call for a premade sauce as their base. Depending on the level of prep work you'd like to do at home and how long you'll be out, you can decide whether you want to use a dried sauce (recipes follow), a fresh sauce, or a prepackaged sauce of one sort or another. For more on sauces and how to arrange ingredients for ease of use on the trail, revisit "Planning Your Trip: Your Backcountry Pantry," page 11. Special instructions are noted as needed in the recipes that follow.

SAUCES AND SEASONING

Dry Alfredo Sauce

Makes: 12 servings	Weight: 0.83 lbs.	V	GF	NF

INGREDIENTS
1 cup powdered milk
¼ cup cornstarch (look for labels reading "GMO-free";
   avoid brands that list MSG or glutamate)
4 teaspoons onion powder
1 teaspoon garlic powder
½ teaspoon salt
½ teaspoon white pepper
2 cups Parmesan powder

Servings	12
PER SERVING	
Calories	**286**
Fat	23g
Protein	13g
Sodium	591mg
Fiber	0g
Carbohydrates	8g
Sugar	4g
Vitamin A: 14% • Vitamin C: 2%	
Calcium: 44% • Iron: 0%	

Reconstituting one ¼-cup (dry) serving
1 tablespoon fresh butter
¼ cup water

Reconstituting entire 3-cup (dry) recipe
¾ cup fresh butter
3 cups hot water

METHOD
Add dry mix, water, and butter. Let sit a couple minutes to thicken.

Dry Marinara Sauce

Makes: 4 servings (1 cup dry) | **Weight: 0.18 lbs.**

INGREDIENTS

4 teaspoons cornstarch (look for labels reading "GMO-free"; avoid brands that list MSG or glutamate)

1 tablespoon onion powder

1 teaspoon garlic powder

2 teaspoons dried parsley

2 teaspoons dried basil

1 teaspoon Italian seasoning

1 teaspoon salt

2 tablespoons sugar

¾ cup tomato powder

Reconstituting one ¼-cup (dry) serving

¾ cup water

Reconstituting entire 1-cup (dry) recipe

3 cups water

METHOD

Add dry mix and water. Let sit a couple minutes to thicken.

Servings	4
PER SERVING	
Calories	43
Fat	0g
Protein	0g
Sodium	1182mg
Fiber	1g
Carbohydrates	11g
Sugar	7g
Vitamin A: 6% • Vitamin C: 8%	
Calcium: 1% • Iron: 2%	

Premix your marinara sauce dry ingredients at home for easy transport. Photo: Sarah Hipple

Dry Pesto Sauce

Makes: 4 servings (½ cup dry) | **Weight: 0.45 lbs.** | V GF

We prefer to make our own fresh pesto, but dried pesto is a decent stand-in for the backcountry, when you don't want to carry the weight.

If you aren't cooking the pesto, mix the water in first and let it sit for several minutes before adding the oil.

Servings	4
PER SERVING	
Calories	569
Fat	52g
Protein	14g
Sodium	700mg
Fiber	5g
Carbohydrates	13g
Sugar	1g
Vitamin A: 21% • Vitamin C: 7%	
Calcium: 81% • Iron: 23%	

INGREDIENTS
¾ cup dried basil
1 cup Parmesan powder
3 tablespoons garlic powder
⅓ cup ground pine nuts or walnuts
½ teaspoon salt

Reconstituting one ½-cup (dry) serving
½ cup water
2 tablespoons olive oil

Reconstituting entire 2-cup (dry) recipe
2 cups water
½ cup olive oil

METHOD
Add dry mix and water. Let sit a couple minutes to thicken. Add olive oil and stir.

Taco Seasoning

Makes: ¼ cup | Weight: 0.07 lbs. | DF | GF | NF

Use this recipe as a substitute for prepackaged seasonings from the grocery store. This seasoning is especially tasty in the burrito and the tortilla soup recipes that follow.

Servings	1
PER SERVING	
Calories	84
Fat	2g
Protein	3g
Sodium	4805mg
Fiber	5g
Carbohydrates	16g
Sugar	1g
Vitamin A: 46% • Vitamin C: 11%	
Calcium: 11% • Iron: 23%	

INGREDIENTS

1 tablespoon onion powder

1 teaspoon garlic powder

2 teaspoons salt

1 tablespoon chili powder

1 teaspoon cornstarch (look for labels reading "GMO-free"; avoid brands that list MSG or glutamate)

2 teaspoons cumin

1 teaspoon oregano

METHOD

Combine all ingredients in a zippered storage bag for use on the trail.

Spice up backcountry meals, from tacos to soups, with this prep-at-home seasoning. Photo: Alan Levine, Creative Commons on Flickr.

BREADS AND WRAPS

Ethan's Bomber Bread

AMC TRAIL-TESTED | **Makes: 1 loaf of bread, or 6 small dinner rolls**

Weight: 0.84 lbs. | DF | GF | NF |

Servings	6
PER SERVING	
Calories	242
Fat	1g
Protein	7g
Sodium	396mg
Fiber	2g
Carbohydrates	51g
Sugar	2g
Vitamin A: 0% • Vitamin C: 0%	
Calcium: 1% • Iron: 16%	

This is our standard backcountry bread recipe. We've used it for years on SCA trail crews and in AMC huts because it's simple, easy to remember, and the result is always satisfying. We often make pull-apart dinner rolls rather than a single loaf that requires a large knife to cut. Use white or wheat flour, but beware of using too high a proportion of whole-wheat flour. Anything with more than 50 percent whole wheat will turn out dense as a brick. And while the tenderness of 100 percent white flour is delicious, the 50-50 blend offers more whole-grain fiber and nutrients without sacrificing taste.

Most bread recipes call for a step where you "proof" the yeast: You combine sugar, water, and yeast in a bowl and wait a couple of minutes to see if the yeast starts bubbling. The bubbles tell you the yeast is still alive and active. If the yeast doesn't bubble, you discard the mixture and use a different yeast. Since you'll be baking in the backcountry, without access to additional yeast, this step is pointless and not included here. The yeast either will be active and your bread will rise, or it won't. There isn't anything you can do about it, so don't worry about it!

INGREDIENTS

1 cup lukewarm water
1 tablespoon yeast or 1 packet instant dry yeast
1 tablespoon sugar
1 teaspoon salt
4 cups flour

METHOD

1. Mix lukewarm water, yeast, sugar, and salt in a bowl or pot. Whisk thoroughly to dissolve ingredients. If water is too hot, it will kill the yeast. If too cold, it won't activate. Lukewarm water is slightly warmer than room temperature but not hot.

2. Add flour 1 cup at a time. The amount of flour will vary by location, altitude, humidity, and temperature, so don't get too hung up on the exact amount. Your goal is to get the dough to form a ball that's the consistency and texture of a baby's bottom. If it's still wet and sticky, add more flour, a few tablespoons at a time. If it's crumbly and dry, add more water, 1 teaspoon at a time. It's easy to overdo it so go slowly.

3. With clean hands, start kneading the dough in the bowl or pot. Kneading is basically a repeated punching and folding of the dough. Fold it in half or in thirds, over and over, and eventually you'll get a rhythm going. The longer you knead, the more tender your bread will be. We usually knead for at least 10 minutes, but longer is better if you have time and energy.

4. After kneading, put the dough (still in the pot or bowl) in a warm location to rise: a sunny rock, next to your stove, or inside your warm tent. If it's cold out and you can't find a warm spot in the sun, put dough in a 1-gallon zippered bag then put that inside a sleeping bag—and get in. With a person inside, the sleeping bag should be right about 98° F—the perfect temperature for yeast to activate and dough to rise. Let dough rise until it doubles in volume or 1 hour has passed, whichever comes first.

5. For a loaf: Punch the risen dough down then start shaping it into a rectangular loaf.

6. For dinner rolls: Punch the risen dough down then break off golf ball-sized pieces and roll them in your hands until smooth. Place them a couple of inches apart on a greased pan or Dutch oven.

7. Let the dough rise for another 20 to 30 minutes after forming in the pan.

8. Bake for 30 to 35 minutes in a greased reflector oven, Dutch oven, or fry-bake pan. You will see steam coming out if using a Dutch oven or fry-bake pan. Don't panic: This is normal. Just keep sniffing the air; if you smell something burning, reduce the bottom heat. The bread is ready when its top is good and golden brown. Let cool for 5 minutes before serving.

Cornbread

INGREDIENTS

½ cup butter powder or melted butter

4 tablespoons egg crystals

⅔ cup sugar

3 tablespoons powdered milk or powdered buttermilk

½ teaspoon baking soda

1 cup cornmeal

1 cup all-purpose flour

½ teaspoon salt

1¾ plus 2 tablespoons water

Servings	12
PER SERVING	
Calories	205
Fat	9g
Protein	3g
Sodium	166mg
Fiber	1g
Carbohydrates	29g
Sugar	12g
Vitamin A: 6% • Vitamin C: 0%	
Calcium: 1% • Iron: 6%	

METHOD

1. Mix all ingredients.

2. Pour into greased fry-bake pan, reflector oven pan, or Dutch oven. Bake for 30 to 35 minutes, or until a toothpick or fork inserted into the middle comes out clean.

Hearty and rugged: two things you and cornbread have in common. Photo: Stone Soup Institute, Creative Commons on Flickr

Bannock

Bannock is a quick-rising bread with both Scottish and American Indian roots. It's basically a leavened flatbread, cooked in a pan or baked. The beauty of bannock—as opposed to a yeasted bread, like Bomber Bread—is there's no waiting for it to rise. Simply mix and bake. Or fry. You can even wrap the dough on a stick and cook it directly over a fire; we call this "firebread." It is incredibly diverse and cooks well in a reflector oven, a fry-bake pan, or a Dutch oven. Add extra ingredients, such as raisins, cheese, blueberries, or nuts, or just leave it plain and slather it with butter and honey. It is very durable and travels well, so if you cook extra at dinner, throw it in your pack and pull it out the next day for lunch. It goes equally well with peanut butter and jelly or salami and cheese.

Servings	4
PER SERVING	
Calories	335
Fat	9g
Protein	7g
Sodium	787mg
Fiber	2g
Carbohydrates	55g
Sugar	0g
Vitamin A: 5% • Vitamin C: 0%	
Calcium: 29% • Iron: 21%	

INGREDIENTS

2 cups all-purpose flour
4 teaspoons baking powder
½ teaspoon salt
3 tablespoons butter powder
Extra ¼ cup flour for kneading
1 cup plus 2 tablespoons water

METHOD

1. *At Home:* Mix all dry ingredients and store in a zippered sandwich bag. Pack extra kneading flour separately.

2. *On the Trail:* Grease a fry-bake pan, reflector oven pan, Dutch oven, or stove-top pan. Mix dry ingredients with water in a bowl. The dough should be wet.

3. Turn dough out onto a floured plate, pot lid, or flexible cutting board. Gently knead about 12 times. If it's too sticky to handle, add extra flour as you're kneading.

4. Form dough into a rough circle as big as whatever you're baking it in, no more than 1½-inch thick.

Fresh bannock in the backcountry conquers cold, rain, and whining. Photo: Marc Chalufour

5. *To bake:* Place in greased pan or oven. Bake for 20 to 25 minutes or until the top gets golden brown and a fork or toothpick inserted into the middle comes out clean.

6. *To fry:* Fry the bannock on a greased stove-top pan over low stove flame or over a bed of coals. After about 10 minutes, flip it over and cook for another 10 to 15 minutes.

7. *To fire:* Scrape the bark off some long twigs, always choosing dead and downed wood. Wrap long, snake-shaped pieces of dough around the sticks. You may need to add extra flour to get the right consistency. Gently hold and rotate over the fire until the bannock is golden brown all over, just like a marshmallow.

Basic Pizza

Makes: 2 small pizzas to feed 4 people **Weight: 2.06 lbs.**

We have made it a family tradition to find the best pizza places near all of our destinations. But why wait until the drive home? You can make delicious pizza in the backcountry. Prepping multiple batches can be time consuming, though, so if you're serving more than two people, plan this for a day when you don't have a lot of miles to cover.

For years we only used mozzarella and Parmesan until we discovered that cheddar adds a savory, nutty flavor to the pie. We'll never go back to plain old mozz again!

Servings	4
PER SERVING	
Calories	935
Fat	45g
Protein	47g
Sodium	2443mg
Fiber	8 g
Carbohydrates	84g
Sugar	22g
Vitamin A: 56% • Vitamin C: 7%	
Calcium: 107% • Iron: 30%	

INGREDIENTS
Ethan's Bomber Bread, substituting all-purpose flour for whole-wheat flour
   (see page 120)
2 cups water, plus extra to rehydrate toppings
½ cup Dry Marinara Sauce mix (see page 117)
½ pound mozzarella cheese, shredded
½ pound cheddar cheese, shredded
½ cup grated Parmesan cheese
Optional: other toppings, such as dehydrated vegetables and meats

METHOD
1. Prepare ingredients for Ethan's Bomber Bread and set aside to rise. For tender dough, let it rise in a warm spot for at least 45 minutes.

2. Boil 2 cups of water, plus extra for any dehydrated toppings; remember you'll need a 1:1 ratio of water to toppings. Pour hot water into sauce mix and stir; rehydrate any toppings.

3. Once dough has risen, punch it down and cut it in half. Each half will make one small pizza crust.

4. Using a flexible cutting board as a work surface, push one dough ball into the shape of a circle ½-inch thick. You could use a floured water bottle as a rolling pin or use the toss-and-spin method. It will take time and patience; just keep at it.

5. Place dough in a greased fry-bake pan, Dutch oven, or reflector oven. Spread half the sauce on the dough and cover liberally with cheeses, followed by any toppings.

6. Bake in fry-bake pan, Dutch oven, or reflector oven for about 15 to 20 minutes. Keep heat low on the bottom and high on the top to get golden brown cheese. Eat, repeat, and enjoy!

Basic Calzones

Makes: 2 calzones to feed 4 people | **Weight: 2.56 lbs.**

V | NF | ⛺ | 🏋

INGREDIENTS

Ethan's Bomber Bread, substituting all-purpose flour for whole-wheat flour (see page 120)

2 cups water, plus extra to rehydrate toppings

½ cup Dry Marinara Sauce mix (see page 117)

½ pound shredded mozzarella cheese

½ pound shredded cheddar cheese

½ cup grated Parmesan cheese

1 cup fresh ricotta or Ricotta Cheese Substitute (see page 149)

Servings	4
PER SERVING	
Calories	879
Fat	48g
Protein	44g
Sodium	1726mg
Fiber	3g
Carbohydrates	60g
Sugar	6g
Vitamin A: 33% • Vitamin C: 1%	
Calcium: 116% • Iron: 7%	

METHOD

1. Prepare ingredients for Ethan's Bomber Bread and set aside to rise. For tender dough, let it rise in a warm spot for at least 45 minutes.

2. Boil 2 cups of water, plus extra for any dehydrated toppings you may want to add later; remember you'll need a 1:1 ratio of water to toppings. Pour 2 cups of hot water into sauce mix and stir; rehydrate any dehydrated toppings.

3. Once the dough has risen, punch it down and cut it in half. Each half will make one small calzone crust.

4. Layer sauce, ricotta, cheese, and toppings on half of each dough circle, leaving a 1-inch gap all the way around the edge. Fold the untopped half of the dough over the toppings and pinch the halves shut along the 1-inch allowance. Wet your fingers if the dough is not bonding together.

5. Bake in a fry-bake pan, Dutch oven, or reflector oven for 15 to 20 minutes or until dough is golden brown. Repeat for second calzone.

Pozole Pie

Serves: 4 to 6   Weight: 3.93 lbs.

This is a savory, Tex-Mex-style layered casserole of cheddar cheese, beans, beef, and tortillas, topped with a thick layer of golden-brown cornbread. Delicious! Because this recipe relies heavily on canned goods, it works best for paddling trips or backpacking trips where you don't mind the extra weight. If you're paddling, bring corn tortilla chips instead of corn tortillas. And do use corn tortillas: Flour tortillas don't have the same flavor.

Servings	6
PER SERVING	
Calories	590
Fat	29g
Protein	23g
Sodium	871mg
Fiber	7g
Carbohydrates	62g
Sugar	15g
Vitamin A: 25% • Vitamin C: 70%	
Calcium: 46% • Iron: 14%	

INGREDIENTS

Filling
1 15-ounce can chili (no beans; organic options exist)
1 15-ounce can pinto beans, drained
1 15-ounce can white hominy or corn, drained
3 tablespoons tomato powder
2 tablespoons onion powder
½ teaspoon dried garlic granules
1 teaspoon chili powder
½ teaspoon cumin
Salt and pepper
1 cup water
6 corn tortillas or 3 cups crushed tortilla chips
¾ pound cheddar cheese, shredded

Cornbread Topping
½ recipe Cornbread (see page 122), dry ingredients only
1 cup water

METHOD

1. Add chili, beans, hominy or corn, tomato powder, onion, garlic, spices, and water in a pot and slowly heat over low flame for 5 minutes, until mix reaches the consistency of chunky spaghetti sauce. Add 1 or 2 tablespoons of water if sauce is too thick.

2. While chili mixture is heating, prepare cornbread mix as directed.

3. Build the pozole pie in your pan or Dutch oven, similar to Baked Lasagna (see page 149), with many thin layers of sauce, tortillas, and cheese. Start with sauce on bottom, followed by tortillas then cheese. Repeat until your ingredients are used up, reserving ¼ cup of shredded cheese for the final step. Leave at least 1 inch of room at top of pan for cornbread.

4. Spread cornbread batter evenly over the top of the pozole pie. (It will bake in place!) Sprinkle reserved cheese over cornbread.

5. Cover your fry-bake pan, Dutch oven, or reflector oven and bake for 30 to 45 minutes, or until contents are hot and cornbread is golden brown.

6. Let cool for at least 5 minutes then serve.

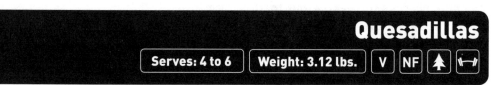

Quesadillas

| Serves: 4 to 6 | Weight: 3.12 lbs. | V | NF | 🌲 | 🏋 |

Quesadillas have always been our go-to meal in the backcountry. Our kids love them, and we rarely go camping without making them at least once. Each quesadilla is made individually, so be prepared to eat them one at a time. Like many things, these can be simple or they can be elaborate. We almost always add refried beans, but whole beans work just as well. If you're having this for dinner on your first night out, bring an avocado and fresh sour cream for a treat. If you're on a paddling trip or somewhere that weight isn't a concern, sauté up some onions and garlic to put inside as well. Yum. Just writing about them makes us hungry.

Servings	6
PER SERVING	
Calories	**697**
Fat	48g
Protein	35g
Sodium	1503mg
Fiber	6g
Carbohydrates	32g
Sugar	3g
Vitamin A: 30% • Vitamin C: 9%	
Calcium: 89% • Iron: 18%	

INGREDIENTS
2 cups dried refried beans
1 cup water
4 tablespoons fresh butter, divided
6 large flour tortillas
1½ pounds cheddar cheese, sliced or shredded; divided
1 cup dried salsa, or a jar of salsa, divided
Sour cream and avocado, optional for garnish

Pro tip: Tortillas and pitas pack and travel better than other premade breads. Photo: Jennifer Wehunt

METHOD

1. To rehydrate refried beans, add hot water to beans, cover, and set aside while preparing first quesadilla.
2. Melt a little less than 1 tablespoon of butter in frying pan.
3. Place a tortilla in pan and spin it around to evenly coat with butter. Flip the tortilla over and coat other side as well.
4. Sprinkle a portion of cheese on one half of the tortilla and spoon some dollops of refried beans over it.
5. Fold tortilla in half and cook on both sides until golden brown and cheese is melted and delicious. Garnish with salsa and other toppings as desired and serve.
6. Repeat for each tortilla.

Burritos

| Serves: 4 to 6 | Weight: 2.91 lbs. | V | NF | | | |

Pretty straightforward stuff here—rice, beans, cheese—but you can spice it up with as much of the extra goodness, below, you want to carry.

Servings	6
PER SERVING	
Calories	**459**
Fat	28g
Protein	24g
Sodium	951mg
Fiber	4g
Carbohydrates	27g
Sugar	1g
Vitamin A: 15% • Vitamin C: 6%	
Calcium: 60% • Iron: 14%	

INGREDIENTS

Mexican Rice (see page 162)
1½ cups dried refried beans, or dried whole beans
2 teaspoons Taco Seasoning (see page 119)
1½ cups boiling water
1 pound cheddar or Monterey Jack cheese, shredded or diced; divided
4 to 6 large flour tortillas
Optional: dehydrated chicken or beef crumbles, onions and peppers to sauté, green chilies, hot sauce, sour cream, salsa, avocado, or guacamole

METHOD

1. Prepare Mexican Rice as directed. Meanwhile, rehydrate beans: Add hot water and Taco Seasoning to beans, stir thoroughly, cover, and let sit for 5 to 7 minutes.

2. Fill each tortilla with Mexican Rice, refried beans, cheese, and any optional additions.

3. Fold sides of tortilla over filling and roll.

Cozy Pigs

Serves: 6 | **Weight: 1.18 lbs. (hot dogs and bannock recipe)** | NF

This one—a campground-friendly recipe—will delight even the youngest kids, but patience is a must to keep the pigs from burning.

Servings	6
PER SERVING	
Calories	296
Fat	21g
Protein	17g
Sodium	1093mg
Fiber	1g
Carbohydrates	43g
Sugar	2 g
Vitamin A: 0% • Vitamin C: 0%	
Calcium: 10% • Iron: 25%	

INGREDIENTS
Bannock (see page 123)
1 package hot dogs (choose options labeled "uncured," "no nitrates added," and "low sodium")
Optional: classic hot dog toppings

METHOD
1. Prepare a batch of Bannock dough as directed. Start a fire and let it burn down to coals.
2. Wrap each hot dog in Bannock dough, making sure dough overlaps at the ends so it all stays together.
3. Skewer your hot dog and cook over the coals to control heat, minimize smoke, and prevent charring. Once rolls are golden brown, dogs are ready.

In the backcountry, bannock is the gift that keeps on giving. Wrap leftover bread around dogs for an easy dinner. Photo: Brian Chow, Creative Commons on Flickr

Gado Gado Noodles in Peanut Sauce

Serves: 4 to 6 | **Weight: 2.76 lbs.** | V | V+ | DF

INGREDIENTS

¼ cup dried onion flakes
½ teaspoon salt
½ teaspoon garlic powder
1½ teaspoons dried chopped ginger
2 tablespoons brown sugar
½ cup powdered coconut milk
3 tablespoons cider vinegar
2 cups peanut butter
2 tablespoons soy sauce or tamari
1 tablespoon oil

Servings	6
PER SERVING	
Calories	659
Fat	38g
Protein	25g
Sodium	681mg
Fiber	7g
Carbohydrates	66g
Sugar	11g
Vitamin A: 13% • Vitamin C: 3%	
Calcium: 7% • Iron: 20%	

Other

¼ cup dried shredded carrots
¼ cup dried peppers
¼ cup dried spinach
1 pound soba noodles, or any pasta of your choice
3 quarts water, or just enough to cover pasta and vegetables

METHOD

1. In a bowl, mix powdered ingredients and wet ingredients.

2. Put dried vegetables and pasta into a pot and cover with water, about 3 quarts. Bring to a boil, remove from heat, and let sit for 10 minutes. Drain; reserve 2 cups pasta water.

3. Pour 2 cups of pasta water into sauce mixture and stir to combine.

4. If sauce is too thick, add more water to reach desired consistency.

5. Stir sauce into pasta and vegetables and serve.

5-Minute Gado Gado

Serves: 1 | Weight: 0.26 lbs. | DF

We spent years leading trail crews for the Student Conservation Association (SCA). After a day of trail work above treeline in the Rockies, afternoon thunderstorms would inevitably roll in and drench our teenage crews. We'd hike back to camp in a downpour and arrive in our high-elevation backcountry camp with everyone tired, cold, and hungry. We needed hot food, and we needed it fast. This single-serve version of Gado Gado noodles is tasty, salty, warm, and incredibly fast to prepare. Nothing will warm you up quicker on a cold day. It works as a snack after a tough day or as dinner itself.

Servings	1
PER SERVING	
Calories	442
Fat	30g
Protein	12g
Sodium	391mg
Fiber	4g
Carbohydrates	35g
Sugar	4g
Vitamin A: 0% • Vitamin C: 0%	
Calcium: 4% • Iron: 15%	

INGREDIENTS

1 package of dry flat noodles (ramen-style or other)
1 bouillon cube (chicken, beef, or vegetable), crushed
2 cups boiling water
2 tablespoons peanut butter
Hot sauce, to taste
Optional: cucumber, crushed peanuts, lime

METHOD

1. Place ramen noodle block in your bowl. Pour boiling water over block. Allow noodles to soak and soften for a couple of minutes. (Don't add seasoning packet yet.)

2. Pour all but 2 tablespoons of water. Add bouillon cube and 2 tablespoons peanut butter to the noodles. Stir thoroughly to make a creamy, delicious instant peanut sauce. Sprinkle with your favorite hot sauce, and you can even spruce it up with fresh slices of cucumber, crushed peanuts, and a slice of lime.

Bowls of edible comfort, noodles are one of the simplest backcountry meals. Photo: Zak Klein

Cauliflower Pine Nut Pasta

| Serves: 6 | Weight: 2 lbs. | V | |

INGREDIENTS

3 quarts water

1 pound penne, or your preferred pasta (make a note
  of cooking time and pack with ingredients)

½ cup currants or raisins

⅓ cup sun-dried tomatoes, chopped
  (not packed in oil)

2 cups dehydrated cauliflower florets, bite-sized,
  or 1 full head of cauliflower

½ teaspoon turmeric

2 tablespoons onion powder

1 teaspoon garlic powder

¼ teaspoon red pepper flakes

1 teaspoon salt

3 tablespoons olive oil

2 tablespoons dried parsley

½ teaspoon dried rosemary

½ cup pine nuts, roasted

1 tablespoon lemon juice, or 1 packet dehydrated lemon juice

1 cup grated Parmesan cheese

Servings	6
PER SERVING	
Calories	583
Fat	4g
Protein	20g
Sodium	545mg
Fiber	6g
Carbohydrates	74g
Sugar	11g
Vitamin A: 6% • Vitamin C: 35%	
Calcium: 22% • Iron: 14%	

METHOD

1. Bring large pot of water to a boil.

2. Put pasta and all ingredients from raisins through salt in the boiling
   water. Cook pasta and drain.

3. Add parsley, rosemary, pine nuts, and lemon juice. Stir to combine.

4. Mix well and serve with grated Parmesan.

Cauliflower is a great source of vitamin C.
Photo: Travis, Creative Commons on Flickr

Chicken and Bacon Cheesy Pasta

Serves: 4 to 6 | **Weight: 1.7 lbs.** | NF

INGREDIENTS

10 pieces precooked bacon, chopped
3 to 4 quarts water
1 pound pasta, any kind
2 cups dehydrated chicken
½ cup butter powder
2 cups Dry Alfredo Sauce, dry ingredients only
(see page 116)
2 chicken bouillon cubes, crushed
½ cup cheddar powder

Servings	6
PER SERVING	
Calories	**836**
Fat	50g
Protein	33g
Sodium	1978mg
Fiber	3g
Carbohydrates	63g
Sugar	5g
Vitamin A: 12% • Vitamin C: 2%	
Calcium: 35% • Iron: 11%	

METHOD

1. Fry up precooked bacon in pot before you start pasta. Set aside.
2. Bring water to a boil and add pasta to same pot.
3. Halfway through boiling the pasta, add dehydrated chicken to pot as well. If you are using canned chicken, add it later, with the sauce.

Pasta with meat delivers carbs and protein, doing double duty for tired bodies. Photo: Oskar Karlin, Creative Commons on Flickr

4. Once pasta is al dente, drain, reserving 2 cups of pasta water for the sauce.
5. Add butter to hot pasta and chicken. Stir to melt and mix in completely.
6. Stir in Dry Alfredo Sauce, bouillon cubes, and cheddar powder.
7. Add reserved water and stir thoroughly. Scrape the mixing spoon, as a lot of sauce powder will stick to it.
8. Cover pot and let sit for 7 to 8 minutes, until sauce thickens. Remove lid, stir in bacon, and serve.

Tortellini Carbonara

| Serves: 4 to 6 | Weight: 1.7 lbs. | NF | |

INGREDIENTS

10 pieces precooked bacon, chopped

3 to 4 quarts water

1 pound tortellini

½ cup dried peas

¼ cup dried onion flakes

½ cup butter powder

2 cups Dry Alfredo Sauce, dry ingredients only (see page 116)

2 chicken bouillon cubes, crushed

Servings	6
PER SERVING	
Calories	715
Fat	49g
Protein	20g
Sodium	2081mg
Fiber	3g
Carbohydrates	49g
Sugar	4g
Vitamin A: 13% • Vitamin C: 7%	
Calcium: 37% • Iron: 9%	

METHOD

1. Fry up precooked bacon in pot before you start pasta. Set aside.

2. Bring water to a boil then add tortellini and vegetables.

3. Boil for 10 minutes or until pasta and vegetables are cooked. Drain, reserving 2 cups of pasta water for sauce.

4. Add butter to hot pasta and vegetables. Stir to melt and mix in completely.

5. Stir in Dry Alfredo Sauce and bouillon cubes.

6. Add reserved water and stir thoroughly. Scrape the mixing spoon, as a lot of the sauce powder will stick to it.

7. Cover pot and let sit for 7 to 8 minutes until sauce thickens. Remove lid, stir in the bacon, and serve.

Penne with Squash, Tomatoes, and Basil

| Serves: 4 to 6 | Weight: 1.6 lbs. | NF |

INGREDIENTS

3 to 4 quarts water

1 pound penne pasta

1 cup dried sliced zucchini and/or summer squash

½ cup chopped sun-dried tomatoes

½ cup butter powder

2 cups Dry Alfredo Sauce, dry ingredients only (see page 116)

2 chicken bouillon cubes, crushed

2 tablespoons dried basil

Servings	6
PER SERVING	
Calories	624
Fat	22g
Protein	17g
Sodium	1727mg
Fiber	4g
Carbohydrates	65g
Sugar	6g
Vitamin A: 12% • Vitamin C: 7%	
Calcium: 31% • Iron: 10%	

METHOD

1. Bring water to a boil then add pasta and vegetables.

2. Boil for 10 minutes or until pasta and vegetables are cooked. Drain, reserving 2 cups of pasta water for sauce.

3. Add butter to hot pasta and vegetables. Stir to melt and mix in completely.

4. Stir in Dry Alfredo Sauce, bouillon cubes, and basil.

5. Add reserved water and stir thoroughly. Scrape the mixing spoon, as a lot of the sauce powder will stick to it.

6. Cover pot and let sit for 7 to 8 minutes until vegetables rehydrate and sauce thickens. Remove lid and serve.

Pasta, squash, and alfredo sauce: a trio made for the outdoors. Photo: Alan Levine, Creative Commons on Flickr

Mushroom Rigatoni

Serves: 4 to 6 | **Weight: 1.6 lbs.** | V NF

INGREDIENTS

3 to 4 quarts water

1 pound rigatoni pasta

1 cup dried sliced mushrooms

¼ cup dried onion flakes

½ cup butter powder

2 cups Dry Alfredo Sauce, dry ingredients only (see page 116)

½ cup Dry Marinara Sauce, dry ingredients only (see page 117)

2 tablespoons dried parsley

Servings	6
PER SERVING	
Calories	**627**
Fat	33g
Protein	17g
Sodium	1535mg
Fiber	4g
Carbohydrates	65g
Sugar	6g
Vitamin A: 12% • Vitamin C: 2%	
Calcium: 30% • Iron: 8%	

METHOD

1. Bring water to a boil then add pasta and vegetables.

2. Boil for 10 minutes or until pasta and vegetables are cooked. Drain, reserving 2 cups of pasta water for sauce.

3. Add butter to hot pasta and vegetables. Stir to melt and mix in completely.

4. Stir in dry sauce mixes and parsley.

5. Add reserved water and stir thoroughly. Scrape the mixing spoon, as a lot of the sauce powder will stick to it.

6. Cover pot and let sit for 7 to 8 minutes until vegetables rehydrate and sauce thickens. Remove lid and serve.

Fettuccine Alfredo

Serves: 4 to 6 | **Weight: 1.5 lbs.** | V NF

INGREDIENTS

3 to 4 quarts water

1 pound fettuccine pasta

½ cup butter powder

2 cup Dry Alfredo Sauce, dry ingredients only (see page 116)

2 tablespoons dried parsley

1 cup Parmesan powder

Servings	6	
PER SERVING		
Calories	**719**	
Fat	40g	
Protein	26g	
Sodium	1919mg	
Fiber	3g	
Carbohydrates	63g	
Sugar	5g	
Vitamin A: 14%	•	Vitamin C: 1%
Calcium: 63%	•	Iron: 9%

METHOD

1. Bring water to a boil then add pasta and vegetables.

2. Boil for 10 minutes or until pasta and vegetables are cooked. Drain, reserving 2 cups of pasta water for sauce.

3. Add butter to hot pasta. Stir to melt and mix in completely.

4. Stir in Dry Alfredo Sauce and parsley.

5. Add reserved water and stir thoroughly. Scrape the mixing spoon, as a lot of the sauce powder will stick to it.

6. Cover pot and let sit for 7 to 8 minutes until vegetables rehydrate and sauce thickens. Remove lid and serve.

A steaming bowl of pasta alfresco warms the hands and the heart. Photo: Jennifer Wehunt

Gnocchi with Browned Butter and Sage

Serves: 4 to 6 | **Weight: 1.4 lbs.** | V NF

INGREDIENTS

3 quarts water
½ teaspoon salt
16 ounces of potato gnocchi
6 tablespoons fresh butter
1 teaspoon red pepper flakes
1 teaspoon dried sage
½ cup Parmesan powder

Servings	4
PER SERVING	
Calories	**364**
Fat	46g
Protein	29g
Sodium	850mg
Fiber	5g
Carbohydrates	21g
Sugar	5g
Vitamin A: 22% • Vitamin C: 5%	
Calcium: 21% • Iron: 5%	

METHOD

1. Bring a large pot of salted water to a boil. Simmer gnocchi until it floats to top of the water (about 2 to 3 minutes) then keep simmering for another 30 seconds to a minute.

2. Remove from heat and drain water, reserving 2 tablespoons of pasta water for sauce.

3. In another pan, heat butter over medium to high flame until butter starts to brown. Butter should smell delightfully nutty. Be careful not to burn it.

4. Add pepper flakes, sage, and reserved pasta water. Stir until smooth, with butter and water well emulsified.

5. Pour butter over gnocchi, add Parmesan, and stir well before serving.

When you need a shot of starch, try gnocchi. Photo: Oskar Karlin, Creative Commons on Flickr

Pesto Pasta with Sun-Dried Tomatoes and Pine Nuts

| Serves: 4 to 6 | Weight: 2 lbs. | V | |

INGREDIENTS

3 quarts water
¾ cup chopped sun-dried tomatoes
1 pound pasta of your choice
¼ cup butter powder
¼ cup olive oil
1 cup Dry Alfredo Sauce, dry ingredients only (see page 116)
1 cup Dry Pesto Sauce (see page 118)
½ cup pine nuts
1 cup Parmesan powder

Servings	4
PER SERVING	
Calories	**776**
Fat	48g
Protein	27g
Sodium	1598mg
Fiber	5g
Carbohydrates	68g
Sugar	6g
Vitamin A: 12% • Vitamin C: 4%	
Calcium: 57% • Iron: 14%	

METHOD

1. Bring water to a boil then add pasta and sun-dried tomatoes.

2. Boil for 10 minutes or until pasta and vegetables are cooked. Drain, reserving 2 cups of pasta water for sauce.

3. Add butter and olive oil to hot pasta. Stir to melt and mix in completely.

4. Stir in dry sauces.

5. Add reserved water and stir thoroughly. Scrape the mixing spoon, as a lot of the sauce powder will stick to it.

6. Cover pot and let sit for 7 to 8 minutes until sauce thickens. Remove lid, stir in pine nuts, top with Parmesan, and serve.

Pesto Pasta with Veggies

Serves: 4 to 6 | **Weight: 2.3 lbs.** | V

INGREDIENTS

2 cups Dry Pesto Sauce, dry ingredients only (see page 118)

4 quarts water, divided

1 pound pasta of your choice

½ cup chopped sun-dried tomatoes

½ cup dried broccoli

¼ cup dried onion flakes

¼ cup dried peppers, chopped

½ cup olive oil

1 cup Parmesan powder

Servings	6
PER SERVING	
Calories	**601**
Fat	36g
Protein	24g
Sodium	959mg
Fiber	4g
Carbohydrates	63g
Sugar	4g
Vitamin A: 8% • Vitamin C: 23%	
Calcium: 49% • Iron: 10%	

METHOD

1. Mix up pesto-sauce powder in a bowl with 2 cups of water. Let sit while you make pasta.

2. Put remaining water in a pot and bring to a boil.

3. Boil pasta and vegetables, stirring occasionally, 8 to 10 minutes or until pasta is done.

4. Add oil to sauce. Pour pesto sauce over pasta.

5. Stir to combine, top with Parmesan, and serve.

Chili Mac

INGREDIENTS

3 quarts water

1 pound macaroni

¼ cup dried onion flakes

¼ cup dried peppers

¼ cup dried chopped tomatoes

2 cups dehydrated ground beef

¼ cup oil

3 cups cheddar cheese, chopped or shredded

1 teaspoon garlic powder

2 tablespoons chili powder

1 tablespoon cumin

½ cup tomato powder

2 tablespoons brown sugar

Servings	6
PER SERVING	
Calories	**655**
Fat	32g
Protein	34g
Sodium	390mg
Fiber	4g
Carbohydrates	58g
Sugar	7g
Vitamin A: 26% • Vitamin C: 8%	
Calcium: 42% • Iron: 26%	

METHOD

1. Bring water to a boil then add pasta, vegetables, and beef.

2. Boil for 10 minutes or until pasta and vegetables are cooked. Drain, reserving 1½ cups of pasta water for sauce.

3. Add oil to hot pasta. Stir to mix in completely.

4. Stir in all spices.

5. Add reserved water and stir thoroughly. Scrape the mixing spoon, as a lot of the sauce powder will stick to it.

6. Cover pot and let sit for 7 to 8 minutes, until vegetables and beef fully rehydrate and sauce thickens. Stir in grated cheese and serve.

Don't worry too much about technique. In the backcountry, a steaming helping of anything will be the best dinner you've ever had. Photo: Oskar Karlin, Creative Commons on Flickr

Serves: 4 to 6	Weight: 2.3 lbs.	NF

This recipe is also great with salmon in place of tuna. Follow the same recipe, substituting one fish for the other.

Servings	6
PER SERVING	
Calories	829
Fat	44g
Protein	39g
Sodium	2075mg
Fiber	4g
Carbohydrates	69g
Sugar	5g
Vitamin A: 16% • Vitamin C: 4%	
Calcium: 64% • Iron: 13%	

INGREDIENTS

3 to 4 quarts water
1 pound egg noodles
¼ cup dried celery
¼ cup dried mushrooms
¼ cup dried peas
½ cup butter powder
2 cup Dry Alfredo Sauce, dry ingredients only (see page 116)
2 tablespoons dried parsley
10 ounces canned tuna
1 cup Parmesan powder

METHOD

1. Bring water to a boil then add pasta and vegetables.
2. Boil for 10 minutes or until pasta and vegetables are cooked. Drain, reserving 2 cups of pasta water for sauce.
3. Add butter to hot pasta. Stir to melt and mix in completely.
4. Stir in Dry Alfredo Sauce and parsley.
5. Add reserved water and stir thoroughly. Scrape the mixing spoon, as a lot of the sauce powder will stick to it.
6. Cover pot and let sit for 7 to 8 minutes until sauce thickens. Remove lid and stir in tuna.
7. Top with Parmesan and serve.

Visit seafoodwatch.org for guidelines on choosing canned tuna. Photo: Jennifer Wehunt

Beef Stroganoff

Serves: 4 to 6 | **Weight: 1.6 lbs.** | NF

INGREDIENTS

3 quarts water

1 pound egg noodles or pasta of your choice

¼ cup dried mushrooms

¼ cup dried onion flakes

2 cups dehydrated ground beef

4 tablespoons butter powder

¾ cup powdered milk

3 tablespoons flour

¼ cup tomato powder

½ teaspoon pepper

4 beef bouillon cubes, crushed

Servings	6
PER SERVING	
Calories	608
Fat	21g
Protein	31g
Sodium	524mg
Fiber	4g
Carbohydrates	74g
Sugar	9g
Vitamin A: 9% • Vitamin C: 5%	
Calcium: 18% • Iron: 18%	

METHOD

1. Bring water to a boil then add pasta, vegetables, and beef.

2. Boil for 10 minutes or until pasta and vegetables are cooked. Drain, reserving 3½ cups of pasta water for sauce.

3. Add butter to hot pasta. Stir to mix in completely.

4. Stir in remaining dry ingredients.

5. Add reserved water and return to heat, stirring thoroughly. Scrape the mixing spoon, as a lot of the sauce powder will stick to it.

6. Cook for 2 minutes then remove from heat again.

7. Cover pot and let sit for 7 to 8 minutes, until vegetables and beef fully rehydrate and sauce thickens. Stir and serve.

Pad Thai

INGREDIENTS

3 quarts water
¼ cup dried shredded carrots
1 teaspoon garlic powder
1 cup dried chicken, dried shrimp, or a combination of
   both
14 ounces stir-fry rice noodles
1 lime
1½ cups dry-roasted peanuts, crushed
½ teaspoon dried red pepper flakes
¼ cup rice vinegar
½ cup brown sugar
½ cup soy sauce or tamari

Servings	6
PER SERVING	
Calories	**698**
Fat	36g
Protein	24g
Sodium	959mg
Fiber	4g
Carbohydrates	63g
Sugar	4g
Vitamin A: 8% • Vitamin C: 23%	
Calcium: 49% • Iron: 10%	

METHOD

1. Bring water to a boil then add carrots, garlic, and chicken or shrimp.

2. Boil for 8 to 10 minutes.

3. Drop rice noodles into boiling water and stir to separate. Cover and remove from heat. Let stand 8 to 10 minutes until everything is soft. Drain.

4. Add sauce ingredients.

5. Halve the lime and squeeze both halves over noodles.

6. Stir in peanuts and serve.

Baked Lasagna

Serves: 4 to 6	Weight: 3.14 lbs.	NF

This is the ultimate, pull-out-all-the-stops, blow-your-mind backcountry meal, perfect for Dutch-oven cooking on paddling trips or via a fry-bake pan on a backpacking trip. It is time consuming and it makes a bit of a mess, but it's worth it for that special occasion when you want to surprise your group with a memorable meal. Nothing else comes close. You'll need either an 8-inch Dutch oven, a 10-inch fry-bake pan, or a 13-inch standard reflector-oven pan. Use the ricotta substitute, below, if you aren't cooking this dish on your first day out.

Servings	6
PER SERVING	
Calories	603
Fat	30g
Protein	40g
Sodium	916mg
Fiber	2g
Carbohydrates	42g
Sugar	4g
Vitamin A: 25% • Vitamin C: 1%	
Calcium: 62% • Iron: 11%	

INGREDIENTS
8 cups water
6 sheets lasagna noodles
1 cup Dry Marinara Sauce mix (see page 117)
1 cup dehydrated ground beef
2 tablespoons dried carrots
1 cup fresh ricotta cheese or Ricotta Cheese Substitute (below)
2 tablespoons egg crystals
¼ teaspoon nutmeg
Salt and pepper
1 pound mozzarella cheese, grated or diced
½ cup Parmesan powder
20 slices pepperoni

Ricotta Cheese Substitute
1 pound firm tofu
Salt and pepper to taste
1 tablespoon vegetable oil

METHOD
1. Boil water and cook noodles for about 7 minutes, until they are just barely al dente. Don't overcook them, as they will continue cooking in the sauce.
2. While noodles are cooking, put Dry Marinara Sauce, beef crumbles, and carrots in a bowl or pot. Put ricotta in a separate bowl. (If using Ricotta

Just like grandma used to make, if she was an outdoorswoman. Photo: Travis, Creative Commons on Flickr

Cheese Substitute, use a fork to combine ingredients until smooth.) If you didn't pack remaining cheeses together, combine them now.

3. When pasta is al dente, drain pasta cooking water, reserving 4¾ cups, and set pasta aside. Pour reserved cooking water into sauce mix while very hot.

4. Stir sauce and let sit for 10 minutes. Wrap pot in a warm layer to retain heat. Add salt and pepper to taste.

5. Stir the ricotta (or substitute) together with egg crystals and nutmeg.

6. In fry-bake pan, Dutch oven, or reflector-oven pan, begin stacking thin layers in the following order: meat sauce, pasta, ricotta, mozzarella. Always start with meat sauce on bottom and end with a solid layer of cheese on top. Layer pepperoni slices on top then sprinkle with Parmesan, just like on a pizza.

7. Bake in fry-bake pan, Dutch oven, or reflector oven for about 30 minutes. All ingredients are already cooked, so baking simply reheats and creates a nice, golden brown crust on top.

8. Once lasagna is steaming hot and golden brown, let cool for 10 minutes to set and stiffen. Serve and enjoy!

Deconstructed Lasagna

| Serves: 4 to 6 | Weight: 2.9 lbs. | NF | |

This recipe is very similar to the Baked Lasagna recipe in this chapter, except we skip all of the baking to make it a one-pot wonder. It might not look pretty, but who's looking anyway? If you're not eating this the first night of the trip, use the Ricotta Cheese Substitute on page 149.

Servings	6
PER SERVING	
Calories	**771**
Fat	35g
Protein	48g
Sodium	1122mg
Fiber	3g
Carbohydrates	65g
Sugar	7g
Vitamin A: 23% • Vitamin C: 1%	
Calcium: 74% • Iron: 14%	

INGREDIENTS
20 slices of pepperoni, cut into quarters
3 to 4 quarts water
1 pound pasta of your choice
1 cup dehydrated ground beef
1 cup Dry Marinara Sauce, dry ingredients only (see page 117)
Salt and pepper to taste
1 cup fresh ricotta cheese, or Ricotta Cheese Substitute (see page 149)
1 pound mozzarella cheese, grated or diced
½ cup Parmesan powder

METHOD
1. Fry pepperoni in bottom of a pot for 3 to 5 minutes, just until it starts to turn golden brown around edges. Remove from pot and set aside.
2. In same pot, bring water to a boil and add pasta and beef.
3. Boil for 8 minutes then remove from heat and drain, reserving all pasta water to use for sauce.
4. Stir Dry Marinara Sauce, salt, and pepper into pasta. Add 3 cups hot water. Mix thoroughly, cover, and let sit for 10 minutes.
5. If using Ricotta Cheese Substitute, use a fork to mash ingredients together until smooth.
6. Stir in three cheeses and pepperoni then serve.

Macaroni and Cheese

Serves: 6	Weight: 2.5 lbs.	V	NF		

This is a classic trail meal and one that is guaranteed to please your hungry, tired hiking buddies after a long and grueling day. Mac and cheese is pretty much known as the ultimate comfort food. Don't be bashful; just embrace the ooey-gooey deliciousness of it. We've even been known to fry up the leftovers for breakfast the next morning.

Servings	6
PER SERVING	
Calories	722
Fat	37g
Protein	31g
Sodium	1142mg
Fiber	3g
Carbohydrates	65g
Sugar	5g
Vitamin A: 22% • Vitamin C: 0%	
Calcium: 61% • Iron: 11%	

INGREDIENTS

3 quarts water
1 teaspoon salt
1 pound elbow macaroni, or pasta of your choice (note package's cook time)
1 pound extra-sharp cheddar cheese, chopped or shredded

Cheese Sauce Mix

5 tablespoons butter powder
6 tablespoons flour
1½ teaspoons dry mustard
¼ teaspoon cayenne pepper (optional)
1 cup powdered milk
1 teaspoon salt
1 teaspoon garlic powder
¼ teaspoon pepper
2 bouillon cubes (chicken or vegetable)

METHOD

1. Bring water and 1 teaspoon salt to a boil. Boil pasta according to package directions. Drain, reserving 5½ cups of pasta water. Cover pasta and set aside.

2. In a new pan, bring reserved water and bouillon cubes to a simmer and fully dissolve.

3. Slowly whisk Cheese Sauce Mix into water, stirring constantly on low to medium flame until slightly thickened.

4. Add cheddar and stir constantly until melted and smooth.

5. Pour cheese sauce over cooked, drained pasta and stir well to incorporate.

6. Cover to keep warm until ready to serve.

Good for dinner, great for breakfast: Fry up mac-and-cheese leftovers. Photo: Oskar Karlin, Creative Commons on Flickr

Buffalo Mac and Cheese

Serves: 6 | Weight: 4 lbs. | NF

INGREDIENTS

Macaroni and Cheese ingredients, page 152
25 ounces canned white-meat chicken, drained and chopped; or dehydrated chicken breast, chopped
½ cup Buffalo wing hot sauce
½ cup blue cheese, crumbled (optional)

Servings	6
PER SERVING	
Calories	801
Fat	40g
Protein	42g
Sodium	1695mg
Fiber	3g
Carbohydrates	66g
Sugar	5g
Vitamin A: 24% • Vitamin C: 23%	
Calcium: 62% • Iron: 15%	

METHOD

1. Prepare Macaroni and Cheese as on page 152, adding chicken and hot sauce to cheese sauce while still in pan.

2. Pour Buffalo chicken and cheese sauce over pot of cooked, drained pasta and stir well to incorporate.

3. Top with crumbled blue cheese if desired.

Bacon and Kale Mac and Cheese

Serves: 6 | Weight: 2.7 lbs. | NF

Precooked bacon is great in this recipe. It doesn't require refrigeration, is very lightweight, and it doesn't make any of the mess you associate with cooking bacon. Kale is also a great addition to mac and cheese.

Servings	6
PER SERVING	
Calories	929
Fat	57g
Protein	37g
Sodium	1526mg
Fiber	3g
Carbohydrates	67g
Sugar	5g
Vitamin A: 74% • Vitamin C: 34%	
Calcium: 64% • Iron: 14%	

INGREDIENTS

Macaroni and Cheese ingredients, page 152
12 slices of precooked bacon, chopped
½ bunch of kale, stemmed and chopped

METHOD

1. Prepare Macaroni and Cheese ingredients as directed, adding chopped kale to boiling pasta about 1 minute before pasta is done cooking. Also, add chopped bacon to cheese sauce.

2. Pour bacon cheese sauce over cooked, drained pasta and kale then stir well to incorporate.

SAVORY CAKES AND RICE

Cheesy Potato Cakes

| Serves: 1 to 2 | Weight: 1.03 lbs. | V | NF | |

Potato pancakes are a great comfort food. This recipe is for a basic cheesy variety, but you can make them into a complete meal by adding meat, such as chopped precooked bacon or canned chicken. If you can bear the weight of fresh cheese instead of powdered, make the switch; the result will be gooey on the inside and extra crisp on the outside.

Servings	2
PER SERVING	
Calories	332
Fat	22g
Protein	7g
Sodium	399mg
Fiber	2g
Carbohydrates	28g
Sugar	0g
Vitamin A: 17% • Vitamin C: 23%	
Calcium: 9% • Iron: 11%	

INGREDIENTS

1⅓ cups dehydrated hash browns
1¼ cup boiling water
2 tablespoons egg crystals
¼ teaspoon garlic powder
Pepper to taste
2 tablespoons dried cheddar cheese
1 tablespoon flour
1 tablespoon dried parsley
3 tablespoons fresh butter

METHOD

1. *At Home:* For ease of preparation once on the trail, pack hash browns in one quart-sized zippered storage bag and the egg crystals, garlic powder, pepper, parsley, flour, and cheddar powder in one snack-sized zippered storage bag.

2. *On the Trail:* Rehydrate hash browns by placing them in a bowl and pouring 1 cup boiling water over top. Cover and let sit for 8 to 10 minutes.

3. Add ¼ cup water to the storage bag containing the egg mixture.

4. Once potatoes are rehydrated, add egg mixture and cheese to the bag and stir to combine. Form patties out of the potatoes.

5. Heat butter in frying pan and place patties in pan. Fry on each side until golden brown.

One whiff of these cheesy potato cakes will bring your group running. Photo: Sarah Hipple

Veggie Potato Cakes

Serves: 1 to 2   **Weight: 1.33 lbs.**   V   NF

For veggie lovers, add any kind of dried vegetables to the potatoes. Be sure to use the right amount of extra water when you are rehydrating them. Be creative. There is no end to the variations you can come up with for this basic recipe.

Servings	2
PER SERVING	
Calories	352
Fat	22g
Protein	8g
Sodium	411mg
Fiber	3g
Carbohydrates	33g
Sugar	2g
Vitamin A: 48% • Vitamin C: 56%	
Calcium: 10% • Iron: 12%	

INGREDIENTS
Cheesy Potato Cakes ingredients, page 155.
¼ cup dried carrots
¼ cup dried peppers
¼ cup dried onion flakes
¼ cup dried zucchini

METHOD

1. Boil water in a pot and cook dried vegetables for 10 minutes. Remove from heat and let sit another 5 minutes.

2. Rehydrate hash browns and egg-and-cheese mixture as directed in Cheesy Potato Cakes (see page 155).

3. Drain vegetables.

4. Once potatoes are rehydrated, add egg-and-cheese mixture and vegetables. Stir to combine. Form patties out of the potatoes.

5. Heat butter in frying pan and place patties in pan. Fry on each side until golden brown.

Sausage and Rice

Serves: 4 to 6 | **Weight: 1.78 lbs.** | DF GF NF

INGREDIENTS

4½ cups water
¼ cup dried peppers
¼ cup dried onion flakes
1 teaspoon garlic powder
4 chicken bouillon cubes
1 teaspoon dried parsley
½ teaspoon salt
¼ teaspoon pepper
2 cups long-grain rice
1 pound summer sausage, sliced

Servings	6
PER SERVING	
Calories	**474**
Fat	21g
Protein	16g
Sodium	1174mg
Fiber	1g
Carbohydrates	53g
Sugar	1g
Vitamin A: 2% • Vitamin C: 11%	
Calcium: 3% • Iron: 21%	

METHOD

1. Bring water to a boil in a pot. Add all ingredients except sausage and return to a boil. Reduce flame to low and cook for 15 minutes, covered.

2. Add sausage slices to pot.

3. Stir then let sit, covered, for 8 to 10 minutes.

4. Fluff with a fork and serve.

Salmon Fried Rice

Serves: 4 | **Weight: 1.69 lbs.** | DF | GF | NF |

INGREDIENTS

5 cups water
¼ cup dried onion flakes
¼ cup dried shredded carrots
1 cup dried shredded cabbage
1 teaspoon garlic powder
1 teaspoon ground ginger
1 tablespoon dried green onions
Salt and pepper to taste
2 cups long-grain rice
2 tablespoons vegetable oil
10 ounces canned salmon (check labels; choose Alaskan pink salmon, sockeye, or red salmon)

Sauce

2 tablespoons soy sauce or tamari
2 tablespoons lemon juice
1 tablespoon brown sugar

Servings	4
PER SERVING	
Calories	**751**
Fat	21g
Protein	51g
Sodium	1135mg
Fiber	2g
Carbohydrates	85g
Sugar	5g
Vitamin A: 29% • Vitamin C: 16%	
Calcium: 44% • Iron: 33%	

METHOD

1. Bring water to a boil in a pot.

2. Add all ingredients except salmon, oil, and sauce, stir well, and cover.

3. Boil for 12 minutes, stir, and let sit, covered, for 8 minutes.

4. Heat oil in a frying pan, add salmon, and cook for 2 minutes. Mix sauce ingredients and pour over salmon, cooking for another few minutes.

5. Spoon rice and vegetable mixture into pan with salmon then stir-fry for 5 to 10 minutes until everything has browned and is well incorporated.

Chicken Cheesy Rice

Serves: 6 | **Weight: 2.15 lbs.** | GF NF

INGREDIENTS

5 cups water
4 tablespoons butter powder
¼ cup dried onion flakes
2 chicken bouillon cubes
¼ cup powdered milk
½ cup dried broccoli
1½ cups dried chicken breast or 25 ounces canned chicken
2 cups long-grain rice
1 pound cheddar cheese or 1 cup cheddar powder

Servings	6
PER SERVING	
Calories	671
Fat	34g
Protein	35g
Sodium	793mg
Fiber	1g
Carbohydrates	52g
Sugar	1g
Vitamin A: 21% • Vitamin C: 13%	
Calcium: 59% • Iron: 19%	

METHOD

1. Put water and butter in a pot and bring to a boil.

2. Add remaining ingredients except cheese, stir well, and cover.

3. Boil for 12 minutes, stir, and let sit, covered, for 8 to 10 minutes.

4. Stir in cheese, combining well, and serve.

When choosing canned salmon, look for Alaskan pink, sockeye, or red varieties. Photo: Zak Klein

Orange Ginger Rice

Serves: 4 to 6 | **Weight: 0.97 lbs.** | V | GF | NF |

INGREDIENTS

5 cups water

4 tablespoons butter powder

1 teaspoon ground ginger

½ teaspoon pepper

2 tablespoons orange juice powder (or double the orange peel, below)

1 teaspoon dehydrated orange peel

¼ cup dried onion flakes

1 teaspoon dried parsley

2 cups long-grain rice

Servings	6
PER SERVING	
Calories	352
Fat	9g
Protein	12g
Sodium	52mg
Fiber	1g
Carbohydrates	53g
Sugar	1g
Vitamin A: 5% • Vitamin C: 5%	
Calcium: 2% • Iron: 17%	

METHOD

1. Bring water and butter to a boil in pot.

2. Add all remaining ingredients, stir well, and cover.

3. Boil for 12 minutes.

4. Remove from heat, stir, cover, and let sit 8 to 10 minutes.

5. Fluff with a fork and serve.

Coconut Rice

Serves: 4 | **Weight: 0.92 lbs.** | V | V+ | DF | GF | NF |

Coconut rice is a great side dish. It goes really well with a stir-fry, if you have any fresh vegetables, or with a can of salmon. Top with some teriyaki sauce, and you've got a delicious meal.

Servings	6
PER SERVING	
Calories	298
Fat	6g
Protein	5g
Sodium	9mg
Fiber	1g
Carbohydrates	54g
Sugar	2g
Vitamin A: 0% • Vitamin C: 0%	
Calcium: 2% • Iron: 21%	

INGREDIENTS

4 cups water
¾ cup powdered coconut milk
1 tablespoon sugar
2 cups rice

METHOD

1. Bring water to a boil in pot.

2. Add all ingredients, stir well, and cover.

3. Boil for 12 minutes.

4. Remove from heat, stir, cover, and let sit 8 to 10 minutes.

5. Fluff with a fork and serve.

Mexican Rice

Serves: 4 | **Weight: 0.91 lbs.** | V | V+ | DF | GF | NF |

INGREDIENTS

4½ cups water
¼ cup oil
2 tablespoons tomato paste
¼ cup dried onion flakes
1 teaspoon garlic powder
4 bouillon cubes (chicken or vegetable), crushed
1 tablespoon dried parsley
¼ cup dried peas
2 cups long-grain rice

Servings	4
PER SERVING	
Calories	**503**
Fat	15g
Protein	8g
Sodium	820mg
Fiber	2g
Carbohydrates	83g
Sugar	3g
Vitamin A: 4% • Vitamin C: 11%	
Calcium: 4% • Iron: 27%	

METHOD

1. Bring water and oil to a boil in pot.

2. Add all ingredients, stir well, and cover.

3. Boil for 12 minutes.

4. Remove from heat, stir, cover, and let sit 8 to 10 minutes.

5. Fluff with a fork and serve.

Rice is as easy to make in the backcountry as at home. Photo: Shaun Dunmall, Creative Commons on Flickr

OTHER GRAINS AND CARBS

Herbed Israeli Couscous with Apples and Cranberries

| Serves: 4 | Weight: 1.9 lbs. | V | V+ | NF |  |

This makes a great dinner and maybe even a better lunch the next day.

INGREDIENTS
2 tablespoons olive oil
2 cups Israeli couscous
4 cups water
4 bouillon cubes (chicken or vegetable), crushed
½ cup chopped dried apple
1 cup dried cranberries
½ cup slivered almonds, toasted

Vinaigrette
¼ cup apple cider vinegar
3 tablespoons maple syrup
¼ cup olive oil
1 teaspoon dried parsley
1 teaspoon dried rosemary
½ teaspoon dried thyme
½ teaspoon salt
½ teaspoon pepper

Servings	4
PER SERVING	
Calories	752
Fat	28g
Protein	14g
Sodium	363mg
Fiber	9g
Carbohydrates	115g
Sugar	36g
Vitamin A: 1% • Vitamin C: 2%	
Calcium: 9% • Iron: 13%	

METHOD
1. In a saucepan, heat olive oil on medium flame. Add couscous and cook, stirring occasionally until slightly brown, about 3 to 5 minutes.
2. Add water, bring to a boil, and add bouillon, dried apple, and cranberries.
3. Simmer 10 to 12 minutes or until liquid has evaporated. Set aside to cool. While pot is cooling, mix all vinaigrette ingredients in a separate bowl.
4. When couscous is cool, pour vinaigrette over top and toss to coat evenly.
5. Add almonds. Enjoy.

Curried Broccoli Couscous

INGREDIENTS

2 quarts water
2 cups Israeli couscous
2 cups dried broccoli
¼ cup chopped sun-dried tomatoes
¼ cup dried shredded carrots
½ cup butter powder
1 cup golden raisins
½ teaspoon crushed red pepper flakes
2 tablespoons curry powder
1 tablespoon garlic powder
Salt and pepper to taste
1 cup cashews, chopped

Servings	4
PER SERVING	
Calories	915
Fat	43g
Protein	23g
Sodium	129mg
Fiber	10g
Carbohydrates	118g
Sugar	27g
Vitamin A: 46% • Vitamin C: 74%	
Calcium: 12% • Iron: 34%	

METHOD

1. In a saucepan, put water on to boil. Add couscous and dried vegetables.
2. Simmer for 10 to 12 minutes or until most of the liquid has evaporated. Drain any remaining liquid and set pot aside.
3. Stir in butter, raisins, spices, and cashews.
4. Let sit for a minute and serve.

Israeli couscous is larger than traditional couscous, closer to tapioca in size. Photo: Jennifer Wehunt

Moroccan Couscous

Serves: 4 to 6 | Weight: 1.25 lbs. | V NF

INGREDIENTS

2½ cups water
2 cups couscous
¼ cup dried onion flakes
¼ cup dried chopped peppers
1¼ teaspoon cumin
⅛ teaspoon ground cloves
½ teaspoon ground ginger
½ teaspoon cardamom
1 teaspoon coriander
⅛ teaspoon cayenne pepper
1 teaspoon salt
½ teaspoon pepper
1 teaspoon orange zest
2 cubes bouillion (chicken or vegetable)
½ cup raisins
¼ cup butter powder

Servings	6
PER SERVING	
Calories	333
Fat	8g
Protein	8g
Sodium	654mg
Fiber	4g
Carbohydrates	56g
Sugar	8g
Vitamin A: 6% • Vitamin C: 11%	
Calcium: 4% • Iron: 7%	

METHOD

1. In a pot, bring water to a boil.
2. Add dried vegetables and herbs then boil for 8 minutes.
3. Remove from heat, and and raisins and butter. Cover.
4. Let sit 8 to 10 minutes, fluff with a fork, and serve.

Couscous with Salmon, Tomatoes, and Zucchini

Serves: 4 to 6 | **Weight: 2.1lbs.** | NF

INGREDIENTS

2¾ cup water
½ cup dried chopped zucchini
½ cup chopped sun-dried tomatoes
4 tablespoons fresh butter
2 cups couscous
¼ teaspoon lemon juice powder
1 teaspoon salt
½ teaspoon pepper
5 to 10 ounces canned salmon (check labels; choose
    Alaskan pink salmon, sockeye, or red salmon)
1 cup Parmesan cheese

Servings	6
PER SERVING	
Calories	538
Fat	22g
Protein	35g
Sodium	477mg
Fiber	4g
Carbohydrates	49g
Sugar	2g
Vitamin A: 12% • Vitamin C: 6%	
Calcium: 48% • Iron: 11%	

METHOD

1. In a pot, bring water to a boil.

2. Add vegetables and boil for 8 minutes.

3. Remove from heat, stir in butter, couscous, lemon juice, salt, and pepper. Stir thoroughly. Cover. Let sit 8 to 10 minutes.

4. Fluff with a fork and add salmon to pot.

5. Sprinkle with Parmesan and serve.

Couscous is a one-pot meal, plate optional. Photo: Batfish Lighting, Creative Commons on Flickr

Steph'z Southwestern "Couz-Couz"

| AMC TRAIL-TESTED | Serves: 2 to 4 | Weight: 1.8 lbs. | V | NF | |

Courtesy of Joe Roman, field coordinator for AMC's backcountry shelters

INGREDIENTS

1 cup water
1 cup couscous
1 15-ounce can black beans, drained
¼ cup salsa, medium
¼ pound cheddar cheese
Hot sauce

METHOD

1. Boil water. Add couscous and black beans.

2. Cover and remove from heat.

3. Let sit for 6 to 8 minutes. Add salsa, cheese, and hot sauce then serve.

Servings	2
PER SERVING	
Calories	567
Fat	7g
Protein	26g
Sodium	915mg
Fiber	16g
Carbohydrates	100g
Sugar	5g
Vitamin A: 5% • Vitamin C: 5%	
Calcium: 21% • Iron: 20%	

Polenta Pizza

Serves: 4 to 6 | Weight: 2.3 lbs. | GF | NF

INGREDIENTS

½ cup of Dry Marinara Sauce, dry ingredients only (see page 117)

1½ cups hot water

18-ounce tube of premade polenta

1 tablespoon olive oil

½ teaspoon garlic powder

Salt and pepper, to taste

1 pound mozzarella cheese, chopped or shredded

20 slices pepperoni

Servings	6
PER SERVING	
Calories	566
Fat	24g
Protein	24g
Sodium	650mg
Fiber	3g
Carbohydrates	63g
Sugar	3g
Vitamin A: 16% • Vitamin C: 1%	
Calcium: 39% • Iron: 21%	

METHOD

1. In a bowl, rehydrate marinara sauce: Add water, stir well, and cover while you prepare the rest of the meal.

2. Slice polenta into ½-inch slices.

3. Heat olive oil in frying pan and place as many slices of polenta in pan as fit, taking care not to overlap. Sprinkle with garlic, salt, and pepper.

4. Let cook without flipping until rounds turn golden brown on the bottom, about 5 minutes. Flip and cook for another 5 minutes.

5. Flip rounds a second time, spread sauce onto rounds, and top with cheese and pepperoni.

6. Cover and continue to cook several minutes, or until cheese melts. Serve.

Serves: 4 to 6 | **Weight: 3 lbs.** | V DF GF NF

INGREDIENTS

1 cup dried black beans
1 cup boiling water
18-ounce tube of premade polenta
½ teaspoon garlic powder
Salt and pepper
1 tablespoon olive oil
2 cups cheddar cheese, chopped or shredded
1 cup salsa

Servings	6
PER SERVING	
Calories	**579**
Fat	17g
Protein	22g
Sodium	501mg
Fiber	9g
Carbohydrates	83g
Sugar	3g
Vitamin A: 13% • Vitamin C: 1%	
Calcium: 33% • Iron: 30%	

METHOD

1. In a bowl, rehydrate dried beans by adding boiling water. Stir well and cover while you prepare the rest of the meal.

2. Heat olive oil in frying pan and place as many slices of polenta in pan as fit, taking care not to overlap. Sprinkle with garlic, salt, and pepper.

3. Let cook without flipping until rounds turn golden brown on the bottom, about 5 minutes. Flip and cook another 5 minutes.

4. Flip rounds a second time, spread sauce onto rounds, and top with cheese and pepperoni.

5. Cover and continue to cook several minutes, or until cheese melts. Serve.

Stuffing with Chicken and Cranberries

Serves: 4 to 6 | **Weight: 1.9 lbs.** | NF

INGREDIENTS

3 cups water
5 tablespoons butter, fresh or powdered
5 cups bread crumbs
1 cup dehydrated chicken
1½ cups dried cranberries

Servings	6
PER SERVING	
Calories	**400**
Fat	13g
Protein	14g
Sodium	749mg
Fiber	3g
Carbohydrates	59g
Sugar	24g
Vitamin A: 7% • Vitamin C: 4%	
Calcium: 4% • Iron: 14%	

METHOD

1. Put water and butter in a pot. Bring to a boil then remove from heat immediately.

2. Stir in remaining ingredients, cover, and let sit for 10 minutes before stirring again and serving.

Thanksgiving in July: Cranberries give dishes vitamins and fiber. Photo: Travis, Creative Commons on Flickr

Stuffing and Sausage

Serves: 4 to 6 | **Weight: 2.7 lbs.** | NF

INGREDIENTS

3 cups water
¼ cup dried onion flakes
¼ cup dried peppers, chopped
5 tablespoons butter, fresh or powdered
5 cups bread crumbs
1 pound summer sausage

Servings	6
PER SERVING	
Calories	**493**
Fat	31g
Protein	17g
Sodium	1195mg
Fiber	1g
Carbohydrates	35g
Sugar	5g
Vitamin A: 8% • Vitamin C: 13%	
Calcium: 4% • Iron: 16%	

METHOD

1. Put water and dried vegetables in a pot. Boil for 5 minutes then add butter.

2. Remove from heat.

3. Stir in stuffing mix, cover, and let sit for 10 minutes before adding the chopped sausage. Stir and serve.

Dinner in the backcountry brings new meaning to "comfort food." Photo: Travis, Creative Commons on Flickr

Cheesy Broccoli, Sausage, and Quinoa

Serves: 4 to 6 | **Weight: 2.9 lbs.** | NF

INGREDIENTS

2 cups quinoa
12 cups water, divided
¼ cup olive oil
¼ cup dried onion flakes
¼ cup dried shredded carrots
1 cup dried broccoli
1 teaspoon garlic powder
4 chicken bouillon cubes, crushed
2 cups cheddar cheese, chopped
1 pound summer sausage, chopped

Sauce Mix

1 teaspoon thyme
Salt and pepper to taste
¼ cup flour
2 tablespoons butter powder
½ cup powdered milk

Servings	6
PER SERVING	
Calories	**791**
Fat	52g
Protein	33g
Sodium	1270mg
Fiber	5g
Carbohydrates	48g
Sugar	6g
Vitamin A: 31% • Vitamin C: 26%	
Calcium: 44% • Iron: 25%	

METHOD

1. Put quinoa in pot and pour 4 cups of water over it. Swirl and swish around vigorously for a couple of minutes. Drain as much water as you can.

2. Measure out 8 cups of water (less if you were unable to drain rinse water completely) and add it to pot, along with oil, vegetables, garlic, and bouillon cubes.

3. Bring to a boil and stir.

4. Reduce flame to medium, cover, and continue to cook for 15 minutes, stirring occasionally.

5. Stir in sauce mix. Continue cooking for one more minute. Remove from heat, add cheese and sausage, and let sit for 5 minutes before stirring and serving.

Quinoa with Pistachios and Dried Cherries

Serves: 4 to 6 | **Weight: 1.3 lbs.** | V | V+ DF GF

INGREDIENTS

2 cups quinoa
8½ cups water, divided
3 tablespoons olive oil
¼ cup dried onion flakes
¾ cup dried cherries, chopped
2 tablespoons dried mint
2 tablespoons dried parsley
Salt and pepper to taste
¾ cup shelled pistachios, chopped

Servings	6
PER SERVING	
Calories	**371**
Fat	17g
Protein	12g
Sodium	20mg
Fiber	6g
Carbohydrates	44g
Sugar	4g
Vitamin A: 5% • Vitamin C: 7%	
Calcium: 7% • Iron: 21%	

METHOD

1. Put quinoa in pot and add 4 cups of water. Swirl and swish it around vigorously then drain as much water as you can.

2. Measure out 4¼ cups of water (less if you were unable to drain rinse water completely) and add it to pot along with oil, onions, cherries, herbs, and salt and pepper.

3. Bring to a boil and stir.

4. Reduce flame to medium, cover, and continue to cook for 15 minutes, stirring occasionally.

5. Remove from heat, stir in nuts, and let sit for 5 minutes before stirring and serving.

Quinoa with pistachios and dried cherries (top right) pairs nicely with (clockwise from center right): falafel, page 180; sweet and spicy rosemary cashews, page 93; bannock, page 123; and no-bake cookies, page 209.
Photo: Marc Chalufour

Almond Sesame Quinoa

Serves: 4 to 6 | **Weight: 0.9 lbs.** | V | V+ | DF | GF |

INGREDIENTS

2 cups quinoa

8 cups of water

2 tablespoons sesame oil

2 packets dried lemon juice

2 tablespoons dried green onions

Salt and pepper to taste

¼ cup slivered almonds, toasted

Servings	6
PER SERVING	
Calories	**272**
Fat	10g
Protein	9g
Sodium	13mg
Fiber	4g
Carbohydrates	37g
Sugar	0g
Vitamin A: 2% • Vitamin C: 1%	
Calcium: 5% • Iron: 15%	

METHOD

1. Put quinoa in pot and add 4 cups of water. Swirl and swish it around vigorously then drain as much water as you can.

2. Measure out 4 cups of water (less if you were unable to drain rinse water completely) and add it to pot along with oil, lemon juice, green onions, and salt and pepper.

3. Bring to a boil and stir.

4. Reduce flame to medium, cover, and continue to cook for 15 minutes, stirring occasionally.

5. Remove from heat, stir in nuts, and let sit for 5 minutes before stirring again and serving.

Cheesy Quinoa with Sweet Potato, Black Beans, and Corn

Serves: 4 to 6 | **Weight: 1.6 lbs.** | V | GF | NF |

INGREDIENTS

2 cups quinoa
9 cups water
1 cup dried, chopped sweet potato
¼ cup dried corn
2 tablespoons dried green onions
½ cup dried black beans
2 teaspoons chili powder
1 teaspoon cumin
Salt and pepper to taste
2 cups cheddar cheese, shredded

Servings	6
PER SERVING	
Calories	462
Fat	17g
Protein	22g
Sodium	270mg
Fiber	8g
Carbohydrates	57g
Sugar	2g
Vitamin A: 77% • Vitamin C: 2%	
Calcium: 34% • Iron: 24%	

METHOD

1. Put quinoa in pot and add 4 cups of water. Swirl and swish it around vigorously then drain as much water as you can.

2. Measure out 5 cups of water (less if you were unable to drain rinse water completely) and add it to pot along with vegetables and seasoning.

3. Bring to a boil and stir.

4. Reduce flame to medium, cover, and continue to cook for 15 minutes, stirring occasionally.

5. Remove from heat and let sit 5 minutes. Sprinkle cheese on top and serve.

Just add grains, water, sweet potato, onion, cheddar, and spices. Photo: Sarah Hipple

Curried Quinoa with Chicken

Serves: 4 | **Weight: 0.75 lbs.** | DF | GF |

INGREDIENTS

2 cups quinoa
9 cups water
2 tablespoons olive oil
¼ cup dried onion flakes
½ teaspoon garlic powder
¼ cup dried red pepper
2 chicken bouillon cubes
1 tablespoon curry powder
1 tablespoon chili powder
1 cup chicken breast, canned or dehydrated
Salt and pepper to taste

Servings	4
PER SERVING	
Calories	**320**
Fat	12g
Protein	19g
Sodium	479mg
Fiber	5g
Carbohydrates	35g
Sugar	1g
Vitamin A: 12% • Vitamin C: 6%	
Calcium: 8% • Iron: 18%	

METHOD

1. Put quinoa in pot and add 4 cups of water. Swirl and swish it around vigorously then drain as much water as you can.

2. Measure out 5 cups of water (less if you were unable to drain rinse water completely) and add it to pot along with oil, vegetables, and seasoning. Bring to a boil.

3. Cover pot and reduce heat to a simmer for 10 to 15 minutes.

4. Add chicken and stir to combine. Turn off heat and keep covered tightly for another 10 minutes.

5. Stir and season to taste with salt and pepper.

"Caretaker's Dream" Stir-Fry

AMC TRAIL-TESTED | **Serves: 2 to 3** | **Weight: 1.48 lbs.**

Courtesy of Joe Roman, field coordinator for AMC's backcountry shelters

INGREDIENTS

1 cup quinoa
2 cups water (or substitute 2 cups broth)
2 tablespoons olive oil
1 head of broccoli, cut into florets
1 green pepper, chopped
1 onion, sliced
1 garlic clove, minced
4 cups fresh spinach, chopped
2 tablespoons soy sauce or tamari
1 tomato, cubed
1 avocado, sliced
Sriracha or other hot sauce, optional

Servings	3
PER SERVING	
Calories	511
Fat	23g
Protein	18g
Sodium	724mg
Fiber	17g
Carbohydrates	65g
Sugar	8g
Vitamin A: 112% • Vitamin C: 398%	
Calcium: 20% • Iron: 34%	

METHOD

1. Put quinoa in pot and add 4 cups of water. Swirl and swish it around vigorously then drain as much water as you can.

2. Measure out 2 cups of water or broth (less if you were unable to drain rinse water completely) and add to quinoa. Bring pot to a boil then cover, turn burner to low, and simmer for 15 minutes.

3. Add oil to separate pan over medium-high flame and stir-fry broccoli, pepper, onion, and garlic until everything is soft.

4. Add a handful of spinach and soy sauce to stir-fry then continue to cook 1 minute longer.

5. Remove from heat and stir in tomato and avocado. Salt to taste.

6. Best served with sriracha or your favorite hot sauce.

The stir-fry is a go-to dish for the caretakers of AMC's backcountry shelters. Photo: Oskar Karlin, Creative Commons on Flickr

Homemade Falafel

INGREDIENTS

Tahini Sauce

½ cup tahini

½ teaspoon garlic powder

1 teaspoon dried lemon juice

¼ teaspoon salt

1 teaspoon dried parsley

¼ cup water

Falafel Mix

2½ cups chickpea flour

1 tablespoon dried parsley

2 teaspoons cumin

1 tablespoon salt

1 teaspoon baking powder

1 teaspoon chili powder

1 teaspoon coriander

2 teaspoons paprika

2 teaspoons garlic powder

1 teaspoon turmeric

1 tablespoon powdered lemon juice

Other

1½ cup water

2 tablespoons vegetable oil

4 to 6 pita breads or gluten-free flatbread

Servings	6
PER SERVING	
Calories	**610**
Fat	22g
Protein	27g
Sodium	1601mg
Fiber	13g
Carbohydrates	76g
Sugar	11g
Vitamin A: 13% • Vitamin C: 5%	
Calcium: 21% • Iron: 45%	

METHOD

1. To make the tahini sauce, mix all tahini sauce ingredients until smooth, adding additional water if needed for a consistency slightly thicker than heavy cream.

2. To make the falafel, bring water to a boil. Slowly whisk falafel mix into boiling water. Stir well, cover, and let sit for 10 minutes until fully rehydrated.

3. Heat oil in frying pan then drop spoonfuls of falafel mix into pan.

4. Fry for several minutes on each side, until nicely browned.

5. Serve falafel patties on pita bread with tahini sauce on top.

Baked Potatoes

Makes: 4 potatoes | **Weight: 1.5 lbs.** | V

So simple and so easy, potatoes are a surprisingly underestimated backpacking food. They're durable, they keep for weeks, and they pack a load of carbs. And they're delicious!

Servings	4
PER SERVING	
Calories	168*
Fat	0g
Protein	5g
Sodium	11mg
Fiber	3g
Carbohydrates	38g
Sugar	1g
Vitamin A: 0% • Vitamin C: 20%	
Calcium: 3% • Iron: 10%	

*Optional toppings will increase calorie count

INGREDIENTS

4 Russet potatoes
Optional toppings: butter, shredded cheese, bacon crumbles, broccoli, or chili

METHOD

1. Start a fire and let it burn down to coals.

2. Make several slits in each potato.

3. Wrap potatoes in two layers of aluminum foil. Nestle in hot coals, turning every 10 minutes or so. Bake for 30 to 40 minutes or until potatoes feel soft when squeezed.

4. Remove potatoes from coals and serve with desired toppings.

Go ahead. Smush them in your pack. Potatoes can take a licking on the trail. Photo: Steven, Creative Commons on Flickr

CURRIES, STEWS, AND SOUPS

Chicken and Veggie Curry

Serves: 4 to 6 | **Weight: 1.4 lbs.** | DF | NF |

INGREDIENTS

7 cups water

2 tablespoons oil

1 5-ounce package of dried noodles (note package's
cook time on package)

¼ cup dried carrots

¼ cup dried onion flakes

½ cup dried chopped cabbage

2 tablespoons curry powder

1 teaspoon sugar

½ cup powdered coconut milk

1 cup chicken breast, canned or dehyrated

Servings	6
PER SERVING	
Calories	451
Fat	21g
Protein	16g
Sodium	242mg
Fiber	3g
Carbohydrates	47g
Sugar	1g
Vitamin A: 16% • Vitamin C: 6%	
Calcium: 3% • Iron: 8%	

METHOD

1. Bring water and oil to a boil. Add vegetables. Let cook for 5 minutes.

2. Add remaining ingredients and continue to cook for another 5 minutes.

3. Stir well and remove from heat.

4. Cover pot and let sit for 7 to 8 minutes, until vegetables fully rehydrate
and sauce thickens. Remove lid and serve.

Taste buds, prepare to drool. Curry is a
backcountry hit. Photo: 185 Scout Group,
Creative Commons on Flickr

Thai Coconut Curry

INGREDIENTS

5 cups water
4 tablespoons butter powder
2 tablespoons curry powder
1 teaspoon sugar
1 cup dehydrated coconut milk
3 vegetable bouillon cubes, crushed
1 pound rice noodles
¼ cup dried onion flakes
¼ cup dried peas
2 tablespoons rice vinegar
½ cup golden raisins
¾ cup cashews, chopped
½ cup shredded coconut (check labels and choose an unsweetened, single-ingredient version)

Servings	6
PER SERVING	
Calories	655
Fat	31g
Protein	10g
Sodium	175mg
Fiber	4g
Carbohydrates	87g
Sugar	11g
Vitamin A: 6% • Vitamin C: 7%	
Calcium: 6% • Iron: 26%	

METHOD

1. Bring water to a boil then add butter, curry powder, sugar, coconut milk, bouillon cubes, vegetables, and rice noodles. Stir well and cook 6 minutes.

2. Cover pot, remove from heat, add rice vinegar, and let sit 7 to 8 minutes, until vegetables fully rehydrate and sauce thickens. Remove lid and stir in raisins and cashews. Serve with coconut sprinkled over each bowl.

Chicken Tikka Masala

Serves: 4 to 6 | **Weight: 1.69 lbs.** | GF NF

INGREDIENTS

5½ cups water
4 tablespoons oil
2 cups long-grain rice
½ cup dried onion flakes
½ cup dried chopped tomatoes
¼ cup dried tomato powder
2 teaspoons garlic powder
1 tablespoon dried chopped ginger
2 tablespoons garam masala
1½ teaspoons cumin
1½ teaspoons coriander
1 teaspoon salt
1 tablespoon sugar
¾ cup powdered milk
1 cup chicken breast, canned or dehydrated

Servings	6
PER SERVING	
Calories	**480**
Fat	15g
Protein	17g
Sodium	553mg
Fiber	2g
Carbohydrates	67g
Sugar	10g
Vitamin A: 6% • Vitamin C: 10%	
Calcium: 18% • Iron: 22%	

METHOD

1. Bring water and oil to a boil then add rice, vegetables, garlic, and ginger.

2. Stir well, cover, and cook for 12 minutes on low flame.

3. Add remaining ingredients to rice and stir.

4. Remove from heat, cover pot, and let sit for 7 to 8 minutes, until vegetables and rice fully rehydrate and sauce thickens. Remove lid, stir, and serve.

Quick Chicken and Rice Stew

Serves: 4 to 6 · **Weight: 0.55 lbs.** · GF · NF ·

INGREDIENTS

9 cups water
1 cup chicken breast, canned or dehydrated
2 vegetable bouillon cubes, crushed
½ cup dehydrated potatoes
1 cup instant rice

Servings	6
PER SERVING	
Calories	253
Fat	2g
Protein	18g
Sodium	125mg
Fiber	5g
Carbohydrates	42g
Sugar	0g
Vitamin A: 96% • Vitamin C: 23%	
Calcium: 4% • Iron: 14%	

METHOD

Bring water to a boil in a pot. Add remaining ingredients and let boil for 1 minute. Cover and remove from heat. Let sit for 10 minutes until everything is rehydrated.

Indonesian Sweet Potato and Cabbage Stew

Serves: 4 to 6 · **Weight: 0.96 lbs.** · V · V+ · DF · 🌲

INGREDIENTS

7½ cups water
1 tablespoon olive oil
½ teaspoon cayenne pepper
1 tablespoon dried chopped ginger
1 teaspoon garlic powder
¼ cup dried onion flakes
1 cup dried diced tomatoes
1 cup dried chopped or dried shredded cabbage
1 cup dried, chopped sweet potatoes
4 vegetable bouillon cubes
½ cup peanut butter
1 tablespoon soy sauce or tamari

Servings	6
PER SERVING	
Calories	193
Fat	16g
Protein	7g
Sodium	300mg
Fiber	3g
Carbohydrates	14g
Sugar	5g
Vitamin A: 70% • Vitamin C: 16%	
Calcium: 4% • Iron: 5%	

METHOD

1. Bring water and oil to a boil in a pot. Add remaining ingredients except peanut butter and soy sauce and let boil for 6 minutes. Cover and remove from heat. Let sit for 10 minutes until everything is rehydrated.

2. Stir in peanut butter and soy sauce until smooth. Serve.

A hearty, healthy stew is a satisfying reward for a day on the trail. Photo: Oskar Karlin, Creative Commons on Flickr

Chili con Carne

Serves: 4 to 6 | **Weight: 1.81 lbs.** | GF NF

INGREDIENTS

5 cups water
1 cup dehydrated ground beef
¼ cup dried onion flakes
¼ cup dried peppers
¼ cup dried corn
½ cup dried chopped tomatoes
1 15-ounce can beans (black, pinto, or kidney), drained
2 tablespoons chili powder
1½ teaspoons garlic powder
1 tablespoon oregano
2 beef bouillon cubes
½ cup tomato powder
2 cups cheddar cheese, chopped or shredded

Servings	6
PER SERVING	
Calories	**316**
Fat	16g
Protein	22g
Sodium	698mg
Fiber	6g
Carbohydrates	20g
Sugar	3g
Vitamin A: 28% • Vitamin C: 20%	
Calcium: 33% • Iron: 14%	

METHOD

1. Bring water to a boil in a pot. Stir in remaining ingredients except cheese and let cook for 8 to 10 minutes.
2. Cover and remove from heat. Let sit for 10 minutes until everything is rehydrated.
3. Stir well and spoon into bowls. Top with cheddar and serve.

One-Pot Deconstructed Enchilada

Serves: 4 to 6 **Weight: 1.68 lbs.** GF NF

INGREDIENTS

4¼ cups water
¼ cup dried onion flakes
¼ cup dried, chopped tomatoes
¼ cup dried corn
¼ cup dried black beans
1 cup dehydrated chicken
1 teaspoon salt
½ teaspoon pepper
3 chicken bouillon cubes
1 teaspoon coriander
1 teaspoon cumin
3 tablespoons chili powder
⅓ cup tomato powder
1½ cups rice
6 corn tortillas, cut into thin strips
2 cups cheddar cheese, chopped or shredded

Servings	6
PER SERVING	
Calories	499
Fat	16g
Protein	25g
Sodium	1098mg
Fiber	6g
Carbohydrates	64g
Sugar	2g
Vitamin A: 33% • Vitamin C: 10%	
Calcium: 34% • Iron: 24%	

METHOD

1. Bring water to a boil. Add all ingredients except tortilla strips and cheese.
2. Stir well, bring back to a boil, cover pot, and cook on low for 15 minutes. Remove from heat and let sit for 5 minutes.
3. Divvy tortilla strips between bowls.
4. Remove pot lid, sprinkle with cheese, and serve on top of tortilla strips.

Chili con carne: good for tailgating,
even better on the trail. Photo: Katie
Bordner, Creative Commons on Flick

Tortilla Soup

Serves: 4 | **Weight: 1.7 lbs.** | GF | NF |

This is one of our favorite soups: filling and very flavorful. The base becomes rich and creamy from whisking the refried beans into the chicken broth. We like to have this on one of the final nights of a trip, to use up the last of our smushed and broken corn tortillas and tortilla chips.

If you are planning to prepare this meal on a paddling trip, or anywhere that weight isn't an issue, substitute canned tomatoes, beans, corn, and salsa. The amounts of each are flexible, as the result will taste great, regardless of exact quantities.

Servings	4
PER SERVING	
Calories	393
Fat	13g
Protein	34g
Sodium	2135mg
Fiber	9g
Carbohydrates	34g
Sugar	5g
Vitamin A: 24% • Vitamin C: 17%	
Calcium: 28% • Iron: 18%	

INGREDIENTS
6½ cups water
½ cup dried diced tomatoes
1 15-ounce can black beans, drained
¼ cup dried corn
¼ cup dried salsa
4 chicken bouillon cubes
¼ cup Taco Seasoning (see page 119)
½ cup dried refried beans
1 cup sharp cheddar cheese, chopped or shredded
1½ cup chicken breast, canned or dehydrated
Corn tortillas, torn into strips, or tortilla chips, to taste

METHOD
1. Bring water to a boil in a pot. Add tomatoes, black beans, corn, chicken, and salsa and let boil for 3 minutes. Cover and remove from heat. Let sit for 10 minutes until everything is rehydrated.
2. Add bouillon cubes, taco seasoning, and refried beans. Stir well to dissolve and fully incorporate flavors. If needed, return to heat.
3. Stir in cheddar and continue stirring until cheese if fully melted and incorporated.
4. Divvy tortilla chips or strips among bowls and spoon hot soup over top.

When tortilla soup is on the menu, plan on seconds and thirds. Photo: Ronald Sikora/AMC Photo Contest

Broccoli and Cheddar Soup

Serves: 4 to 6 | **Weight: 1.6 lbs.** | NF |

INGREDIENTS

4 cups water
¼ cup butter powder
¼ cup flour
1 cup powdered milk
½ teaspoon salt
¼ teaspoon pepper
2 chicken bouillon cubes
¼ cup dried onion flakes
2 tablespoons dried chopped celery
¼ cup dried shredded carrots
¾ cup dried broccoli
2½ cups cheddar cheese, shredded

Servings	6
PER SERVING	
Calories	394
Fat	29g
Protein	19g
Sodium	831mg
Fiber	1g
Carbohydrates	15g
Sugar	9g
Vitamin A: 35% • Vitamin C: 21%	
Calcium: 55% • Iron: 5%	

METHOD

1. Bring water and butter to a boil in a pot. Add all other ingredients except cheese and let boil for 6 minutes. Cover and remove from heat. Let sit for 10 minutes until everything is rehydrated.

2. Stir in cheddar and continue stirring until cheese is fully melted and incorporated. Serve.

Cuban Black Bean Soup

Serves: 4 to 6 | Weight: 2.34 lbs. | DF | GF | NF

INGREDIENTS

6 cups water
3 tablespoons olive oil
6 slices precooked bacon
¼ cup dried onion flakes
¼ cup dried peppers, chopped
1 tablespoon garlic powder
1 tablespoon cumin
1 teaspoon oregano
1 teaspoon salt
⅛ teaspoon cloves
2 chicken bouillon cubes
1 tablespoon tomato powder or paste
2 15-ounce cans black beans, drained
Optional: lime and sour cream for garnish

Servings	6
PER SERVING	
Calories	338
Fat	22g
Protein	11g
Sodium	1270mg
Fiber	8g
Carbohydrates	25g
Sugar	4g
Vitamin A: 4% • Vitamin C: 18%	
Calcium: 10% • Iron: 15%	

METHOD

1. Bring water, oil, and bacon to a boil in a pot. Add remaining ingredients and boil for 6 minutes. Cover and remove from heat. Let sit for 10 minutes until everything is rehydrated and soup thickens.

2. Serve with wedges of fresh lime and sour cream, if desired.

Lentil Soup

Lentils are great trail food, but you have to cook them well, as undercooked lentils will give you a bellyache. Keep adding water if they aren't softening. The good news: You can make this recipe thick and stewlike, or thin and brothy. It's entirely up to your taste.

Servings	4
PER SERVING	
Calories	347
Fat	8g
Protein	20g
Sodium	778mg
Fiber	23g
Carbohydrates	48g
Sugar	4g
Vitamin A: 25% • Vitamin C: 8%	
Calcium: 10% • Iron: 40%	

INGREDIENTS

8 cups water
2 tablespoons olive oil
1½ cups lentils (red or green)
2 tablespoons dried onion flakes
1 teaspoon garlic powder
¼ cup dried chopped carrots
¼ cup dried chopped celery
1 teaspoon rosemary
2 teaspoons thyme
4 bouillon cubes (chicken or vegetable)
2 teaspoons cumin
1 teaspoon oregano
½ teaspoon pepper
2 tablespoons balsamic vinegar

METHOD

1. Bring water and oil to a boil in a pot. Add remaining ingredients to pot and let boil for 1 minute.

2. Cover and reduce heat to a simmer for 15 minutes. Check to see if lentils are soft.

3. If lentils are still a little underdone and water is mostly gone, add more water and continue cooking until lentils are soft.

As good for cold weather as it is for a cold, soup warms up hikers quickly. Photo: Zak Klein

Creamed Chipped Beef

| Serves: 4 to 6 | Weight: 2.04 lbs. | NF |

INGREDIENTS

5 ounces dehydrated beef, sliced into ¼-inch strips

7½ cups water, divided

½ cup butter powder

2 cups powdered milk

¾ cups flour

½ teaspoon salt

Pepper to taste

4 to 6 pita breads, gluten-free flatbread, or any bread you have handy

Servings	6
PER SERVING	
Calories	**516**
Fat	28g
Protein	23g
Sodium	1167mg
Fiber	1g
Carbohydrates	45g
Sugar	17g
Vitamin A: 17% • Vitamin C: 6%	
Calcium: 43% • Iron: 12%	

METHOD

1. Soak dried beef in 2 cups of water while preparing the sauce. Soaking removes some of the salt from the beef and softens it up.

2. Measure 5½ cups of water and bring to a boil in a pot.

3. Add dry ingredients to frying pan then slowly pour in boiling water, whisking vigorously to prevent lumps.

4. Add beef, stir, and cover.

5. Warm pitas on both sides in frying pan.

6. Serve over warmed bread or crackers.

Lemon Butter Trout

Serves: 1 | **Weight: about 0.1 lbs., excluding the fish** | NF

This is a classic method for cooking fresh trout or salmon in the backcountry.

INGREDIENTS

2 tablespoons flour

½ teaspoon salt

Plenty of pepper to taste

About 8 ounces fresh trout fillets (or whole fish)

2 tablespoons fresh butter

Lemon slices or powdered lemon juice, rehydrated

Servings	1
PER SERVING	
Calories	**509**
Fat	35g
Protein	37g
Sodium	1270mg
Fiber	0g
Carbohydrates	12g
Sugar	0g
Vitamin A: 16% • Vitamin C: 1%	
Calcium: 8% • Iron: 18%	

METHOD

1. Mix flour, salt, and pepper then dredge fish fillet in the mixture.

2. Heat butter in a pan over medium flame.

3. Lay flour-dredged fillets in butter, skin-side up if leaving skin on.

4. Cook 2 to 3 minutes then flip.

5. Cook another 2 minutes then remove from heat to check. Fish is done when it is flaky and white, not translucent.

6. Drizzle with leftover cooking butter and browned bits, spritz with lemon, and serve with rice or potatoes, such as Potato Pancakes (see page 155).

Garlic and Thyme Fish on a Stick

| Serves: 1 | Weight: about 0.1 lb., excluding the fish |

Simple and easy, this might be the most primitive way to cook a fish—but it's also delicious.

INGREDIENTS
2 garlic cloves
1 whole trout, gutted and cleaned, head and tail intact
1 teaspoon dried thyme
Salt and pepper
Lemon slices or powdered lemon juice, rehydrated

Servings	1
PER SERVING	
Calories	129
Fat	5g
Protein	17g
Sodium	43mg
Fiber	0g
Carbohydrates	3g
Sugar	0g
Vitamin A: 2% • Vitamin C: 5%	
Calcium: 6% • Iron: 14%	

METHOD
1. Build a fire and let it burn down to coals. Place two flat rocks on either side of the coals, about 10 to 12 inches apart. Tops of rocks should be about 6 to 8 inches above surface of coals.
2. Crush garlic and stuff two cloves in body cavity of fish.
3. Sprinkle thyme over the fish, and season generously with salt and pepper, inside and out.
4. Turn the garlic-stuffed fish upside down, cut-open belly facing you. With a sharp knife, poke a hole through both sides of the belly flaps. Repeat the hole-poking every 2 or 3 inches along the belly of the fish, eventually ending up with 3 to 4 holes poked in the belly flesh, from head to tail.
5. Weave a metal skewer through the holes, making sure the skewer extends at least 4 inches on either end.
6. Place the ends of the stick on the rocks in the fire, so the fish is hanging belly-up directly over the coals, like a rotisserie. Remember: The fire should already be burned down to hot coals, with no flame present.
7. Cook, turning as necessary, for 10 minutes or until fish is flaky and white.
8. Sprinkle with lemon and enjoy!

Knowing the size and bag limits along your route lets you fish responsibly. Photo: Jennifer Wehunt

Trout Piccata

When you want to pull out all the stops!

INGREDIENTS

4 fresh trout fillets
2 teaspoons dried rosemary, ground finely and divided
6 tablespoons flour
2 teaspoons salt
Plenty of pepper to taste
4 tablespoons fresh butter
2 small shallots, finely diced
¾ cup white wine (optional)
Juice from ½ lemon or 1 tablespoon lemon juice
    powder, rehydrated
1 tablespoon capers, drained

METHOD

1. Rub 1 teaspoon rosemary deep into the flesh of the fish.

2. Mix flour, salt, and pepper then dredge fish fillets in the mixture.

3. Heat butter in a pan over medium flame then lay fillets in butter, skin-side up if leaving skin on.

4. Cook 2 or 3 minutes then flip.

5. Cook another 2 minutes on second side then remove from heat to check. Fish is done when it is flaky and white, not translucent. Remove fish from pan and set aside.

6. Throw shallots in remaining butter and fish grease. Sauté for 30 seconds.

7. Pour in wine and scrape up all browned bits. Cook for about 5 minutes until sauce reduces to about ⅓ cup.

8. Stir in lemon juice, capers, and remaining rosemary.

9. Salt and pepper to taste then pour sauce over fish.

10. Serve with rice, fried potatoes, or Unstuffed Peppers (see page 200).

WITHOUT WINE	
Servings	2
PER SERVING	
Calories	538
Fat	32g
Protein	36g
Sodium	2573mg
Fiber	2g
Carbohydrates	22g
Sugar	0g
Vitamin A: 19% • Vitamin C: 17%	
Calcium: 10% • Iron: 23%	

WITH WINE	
Servings	2
PER SERVING	
Calories	610
Fat	33g
Protein	36g
Sodium	2577mg
Fiber	2g
Carbohydrates	24g
Sugar	1g
Vitamin A: 19% • Vitamin C: 17%	
Calcium:11% • Iron: 24%	

Hobo Dinner

Serves: 4

Weight: 2.84 lbs. (dehydrated beef) or 3.56 lbs. (fresh beef)

GF NF

Dinner cooked in the fire! This standby is best at the trailhead using fresh meat, or use meat frozen at home for your first night on the trail. Bring beef, turkey, pork—whatever ground meat suits your group—or go veggie.

INGREDIENTS

1 onion, thinly sliced

4 small potatoes, peeled and thinly sliced

4 carrots, peeled and thinly sliced

1 pound ground meat, or 2 cups dehydrated ground meat plus 2 cups water to rehydrate

Fresh butter

Salt and pepper

Optional: Worcestershire sauce

Servings	4
PER SERVING	
Calories	406
Fat	17g
Protein	26g
Sodium	136mg
Fiber	7g
Carbohydrates	36g
Sugar	7g
Vitamin A: 244% • Vitamin C: 66%	
Calcium: 6% • Iron: 20%	

Wrap hobo dinners in foil and stash them in the coals to cook. Photo: Travis, Creative Commons on Flickr

METHOD

1. Start a fire and let it burn down to coals. Meanwhile, rehydrate ground meat by pouring 2 cups of boiling water over it in a bowl. Cover and let sit for 8 to 10 minutes.

2. Set out 1 square foot of heavy-duty aluminum foil for each person. On each piece of foil, layer in the following, from bottom to top: onions, ¼ of the ground meat, potatoes, carrots (or other vegetables), and butter.

3. Salt and pepper generously. Worcestershire sauce is also a good addition. Seasoning is key!

4. Wrap it all up to make a foil packet, but don't just scrunch the foil together, as it will leak. Bring the edges together then neatly fold them in on themselves once or twice. A second layer of foil will keep the food from scorching.

5. Bury in medium-hot coals and cook for about 40 minutes. Then dig pouch out of coals and unwrap to check if it is fully cooked. If it's not done, put it back on the fire and check every 5 minutes.

Unstuffed Peppers with Beef

| Serves: 4 to 6 | Weight: 2.3 lbs. | GF | NF | | |

INGREDIENTS

5½ cups water
4 tablespoons fresh butter
¾ cup tomato powder
½ cup dried onion flakes
½ cup dried peppers
1 teaspoon garlic powder
Salt and pepper to taste
1 tablespoon sugar
1½ cups dehydrated ground beef
2 cups long-grain rice
1 pound cheddar cheese or 1 cup cheddar powder

Servings	6
PER SERVING	
Calories	609
Fat	32g
Protein	30g
Sodium	432mg
Fiber	1g
Carbohydrates	49g
Sugar	3g
Vitamin A: 21% • Vitamin C: 20%	
Calcium: 49% • Iron: 21%	

METHOD

1. Bring water and butter to a boil in pot.

2. Add all remaining ingredients except cheese, stir well, and cover.

3. Boil for 12 minutes, stir, cover, and let sit for 8 to 10 minutes.

4. Stir in cheese and serve.

Frozen Steaks Alfresco

| Serves: 1 | Weight: 0.75 lbs. | GF | NF | |

This family tradition dates back to our college days in northern Arizona. When heading out on a climbing or a canyoneering trip, we'd splurge on a couple of steaks to freeze at home then pack in our packs. After our first day of hiking deep into the secluded canyon country of the Mogollon Rim, we'd build a small fire near the creek bed and pull out our steaks. They'd often still be frozen, even in 90° F heat. As the sun set, the cicadas would start humming, and the stars would glide overhead. We'd throw a baked potato or two in the coals. A box of red wine would appear from someone's pack, a backpacking guitar from someone else's. Steaks sizzling over the fire, creek babbling peacefully by, wine warming our spirits, music filling the canyons: Life doesn't get much better than these simple moments of food, friends, family, and fresh air.

Servings	1
PER SERVING	
Calories	542
Fat	22g
Protein	73g
Sodium	259mg
Fiber	9g
Carbohydrates	16g
Sugar	1g
Vitamin A: 3% • Vitamin C: 36%	
Calcium: 19% • Iron: 63%	

INGREDIENTS
¾-pound steak, your choice of cut
4 cloves
Salt and pepper to taste

METHOD
1. *At Home:* Freeze the steak then bury it deep in your pack to keep it insulated.
2. *In the Field:* Build up a bed of hot coals. Place your grill 6 to 8 inches above the coals.
3. Cut slits in the meat then stuff with garlic cloves. The cloves will flavor the meat as they sizzle in the steak fat.
4. Season with salt and pepper to taste. A crust of salt makes a fine steak.
5. Grill 3 to 5 minutes per side. Remove from heat and let meat rest for a few minutes before serving.

DESSERTS AND SWEET DRINKS

Not every day in the backcountry allows for the luxury of dessert, but sugar and fat can be key to getting and staying warm in the coldest weather—or just improving morale after a long, hard day. Some of these treats will travel with you in your pack; others you can make in the field for a warm, decadent surprise. As with everything in your backcountry kitchen, a little planning and effort goes a long way toward creating a delectable experience.

Whatever type of trip we're on, there's always a time of day when it's "hot brew" time. Just boil up a pot of water, retrieve your ladle and your bag of hot brew mixes, and let everyone mix and match their favorite drinks. Nothing beats sitting around the fire after dinner, sipping a hot brew, and watching the stars go by overhead or the river flow past below. And when the rain starts falling and the wind starts howling, nothing cheers up a group like sipping cups of hot brew safe in tents or beneath a tarp. Beverages hydrate you, of course, but a psychological shift occurs when you taste that hot brew and cradle a warm mug in your hands. We think of it like backcountry happy hour: a time to come together, sit back, enjoy a hot treat, and discuss the day.

DESERTS

Scotch-a-Roos

| Makes: 30 bars | Weight: 3.5 lbs. | V | GF | |

INGREDIENTS

6 cups puffed rice cereal

1 cup sugar

1 cup corn syrup (look for non-GMO and non-high-fructose varieties, or substitute with the replacement of your choice; e.g., cane syrup)

1 cup peanut butter

2 cups butterscotch chips

2 cups chocolate chips

Servings	30
PER SERVING	
Calories	284
Fat	12g
Protein	4g
Sodium	90mg
Fiber	3g
Carbohydrates	42g
Sugar	27g
Vitamin A: 3% • Vitamin C: 6%	
Calcium: 2% • Iron: 16%	

METHOD

1. Line a 9-by-13-inch baking pan with parchment paper.

2. Measure rice cereal into a large, heat-resistant bowl and set aside.

3. In medium saucepan, combine sugar and corn syrup over medium heat.

4. Once mixture comes to a boil, remove from heat and add peanut butter. Stir until smooth.

5. Add hot peanut butter mix to rice cereal and stir to fully incorporate.

6. Pour mixture into prepared pan, pressing into all edges and corners.

7. Over low heat, melt chocolate chips then add butterscotch chips and stir until smooth. Be sure to melt chocolate first then butterscotch. Melting them together won't produce as smooth a result.

8. Spread chocolate mix over the cereal layer already in the pan and let cool before cutting. Wrap tightly and store in a cool, dark place in your pack for up to 5 days.

Trail Mix Cookies

Makes: 3 dozen | Weight: 3.26 lbs. | V

INGREDIENTS

1 cup fresh butter
1 cup brown sugar
½ cup sugar
2 eggs
1 tablespoon vanilla extract
1¼ cups flour
½ teaspoon baking soda
1 teaspoon salt
3 cups quick oats
1 cup chopped walnuts
1 cup chocolate chips
1 cup raisins

Servings	18
PER SERVING	
Calories	383
Fat	19g
Protein	5g
Sodium	181mg
Fiber	3g
Carbohydrates	49g
Sugar	29g
Vitamin A: 7% • Vitamin C: 1%	
Calcium: 4% • Iron: 10%	

METHOD

1. Preheat oven to 325° F.

2. In a large bowl, cream together butter, brown sugar, and sugar until smooth. Beat in eggs one at a time then stir in vanilla.

3. In another bowl, combine flour, baking soda, and salt. Stir dry mix into creamed mixture until blended. Mix in oats, nuts, chocolate chips, and raisins. Scoop heaping spoonfuls onto a baking sheet.

4. Bake for 12 minutes. Allow cookies to cool on baking sheet for 5 minutes before transferring to a wire rack to cool completely.

5. Store in airtight container for up to 5 days.

After a long day on the trail, lots of hikers turn into cookie monsters. Pack accordingly. Photo: Phoebe, Creative Commons on Flickr

Peanut Butter Squares

| AMC TRAIL-TESTED | Makes: 18 squares | Weight: 3.48 lbs. |

Courtesy of Joe Roman, field coordinator for AMC's backcountry shelters

This recipe requires no baking—a great treat to make if you'll be celebrating a special occasion in the backcountry or if you know you'll be craving an insanely yummy dessert. If you make it in your frying pan after cleaning up from dinner, it will set up and you can cut up the squares for a trail treat the next day. If you don't want to go through the hassle of making these on the trail, just make them at home and hope they don't all get eaten before your trip starts.

Servings	18
PER SERVING	
Calories	496
Fat	28g
Protein	8g
Sodium	137mg
Fiber	3g
Carbohydrates	57g
Sugar	51g
Vitamin A: 5% • Vitamin C: 0%	
Calcium: 3 % • Iron: 8%	

INGREDIENTS

1 cup brown sugar
3½ cups powdered sugar
10 tablespoons butter
2 cups peanut butter
2 cups semisweet chocolate chips
1 tablespoon butter

METHOD

1. Stir first four ingredients, mixing together until smooth and well blended.

2. If making at home, pat into a buttered 9-by-13-inch pan. On the trail, pat into a buttered frying pan.

3. Melt chocolate chips and butter in a pot on very low heat.

4. Spread chocolate over peanut butter mixture and let cool. Cut into squares before chocolate has fully hardened; otherwise, these are tricky to get out of the pan. Once cut, remove from pan.

5. Store in a rigid container for up to 5 days to avoid these getting smushed in a pack and making a mess.

Oatmeal Chocolate Peanut Butter Cookies

Makes: 30 cookies | **Weight: 4.12 lbs.** | V | GF

These hearty cookies are great for the trail if you can restrain yourself from eating them all before you leave home. They're chunky, chewy, and packed with flavor. Oatmeal stands in for flour, so they're easy to make without gluten if you buy gluten-free oats.

Servings	30
PER SERVING	
Calories	353
Fat	15g
Protein	6g
Sodium	165mg
Fiber	3g
Carbohydrates	50g
Sugar	33g
Vitamin A: 3% • Vitamin C: 0%	
Calcium: 36% • Iron: 7%	

INGREDIENTS

½ cup fresh butter

1 cup sugar

1 cup brown sugar

3 eggs

1 teaspoon vanilla

1½ cup crunchy peanut butter

2 tablespoons corn syrup (look for non-GMO and non-high-fructose varieties, or sub in the replacement of your choice; e.g., cane syrup)

2 teaspoons baking soda

5 cups rolled oats

4 cups semisweet chocolate chips

METHOD

1. Preheat oven to 325° F. Line a cookie sheet with parchment paper.

2. Cream butter with both sugars then gradually add eggs.

3. Stir in vanilla, peanut butter, corn syrup, and baking soda. Mix well.

4. Add oats and thoroughly combine before folding in chocolate chips.

5. Measure out ¼-cup balls of dough and place them 2 to 3 inches apart on baking sheet.

6. Bake for 15 minutes or until cookies are golden around edges. Cool on wire rack.

7. Store in airtight container for up to 5 days.

No-Bake Cookies

These cookies are quick, easy, and delicious. You can make them at home or, if you bring some shelf-stable milk, such as Parmalat, you can make them anywhere.

Servings	24
PER SERVING	
Calories	207
Fat	10g
Protein	4g
Sodium	65mg
Fiber	2g
Carbohydrates	27g
Sugar	18g
Vitamin A: 3% • Vitamin C: 0%	
Calcium: 2% • Iron: 4%	

INGREDIENTS

2 cups sugar

½ cup fresh milk (don't substitute dehydrated)

8 tablespoons butter powder

¼ cup cocoa powder

3 cups rolled oats

1 cup peanut butter

1 tablespoon vanilla

⅛ teaspoon salt

METHOD

1. Line a baking sheet with parchment paper.

2. Bring sugar, milk, butter, and cocoa powder to a boil in a saucepan over medium heat, stirring frequently.

3. Let boil for 1 minute then remove from heat.

4. Add oats, peanut butter, vanilla, and salt then stir to combine.

5. Scoop teaspoonfuls onto baking sheet and let cool until hard.

6. Store in airtight container for up to 5 days.

Make these at home then store them in an airtight container for a decadent treat on the trail.
Photo: Marc Chalufour

Caramel Corn

INGREDIENTS

3 quarts popped popcorn

½ cup fresh butter

1 cup brown sugar

¼ cup corn syrup (look for non-GMO and non-high-fructose varieties, or substitute with the replacement of your choice; e.g., cane syrup)

½ teaspoon salt

¼ teaspoon baking soda

1 teaspoon vanilla extract

Servings	12
PER SERVING	
Calories	190
Fat	8g
Protein	1g
Sodium	136mg
Fiber	1g
Carbohydrates	30g
Sugar	20g
Vitamin A: 5% • Vitamin C: 0%	
Calcium: 2% • Iron: 4%	

METHOD

1. Preheat oven to 250° F.

2. Place popcorn in a large bowl.

3. In a saucepan over medium heat, melt butter. Stir in brown sugar, corn syrup, and salt. This is your caramel.

4. Bring to a boil, stirring constantly. Once at a boil, stop stirring, and cook for 4 minutes.

5. Remove from heat and stir in baking soda and vanilla.

6. Pour caramel mix over popcorn, stirring to coat.

7. Pour popcorn onto two large baking sheets, and bake for 1 hour, stirring every 15 minutes. Remove from oven and let cool completely before breaking apart.

8. Store in airtight container for up to 5 days.

Sopapillas

INGREDIENTS

½ cup fresh butter
1 teaspoon cinnamon
¼ cup sugar
1 tablespoon honey
4 tablespoons vegetable oil
4 flour tortillas

Servings	4
PER SERVING	
Calories	483
Fat	39g
Protein	3g
Sodium	194mg
Fiber	1g
Carbohydrates	33g
Sugar	18g
Vitamin A: 14% • Vitamin C: 0%	
Calcium: 5% • Iron: 6%	

METHOD

1. In saucepan, melt butter with cinnamon, sugar, and honey. Stir until sugar is dissolved and mixture is smooth. Set aside.

2. Heat oil in frying pan and cook one tortilla at a time until golden brown and puffy on each side.

3. Remove each tortilla and serve with warm syrup on top.

If you can afford the weight, a Dutch oven does desserts justice. Photo: Travis, Creative Commons on Flickr

Pineapple Upside-Down Cake

Serves: 8 | **Weight: 2.48 lbs.** | V NF

You can bake any cake in a Dutch oven, fry-bake pan, or reflector oven. So if you can make any cake, why not make the most spectacular, mind-blowing, caramely sweet, fruity-good pineapple upside-down cake? We've made this on backpacking and paddling trips, dozens of miles from the nearest road, and it never ceases to delight. The leftover slices can get fried up with butter for a delicious breakfast! Save the pineapple juice you drain as a treat, but remember to press out as much liquid as possible or your cake will get soupy.

Servings	8
PER SERVING	
Calories	**474**
Fat	20g
Protein	3g
Sodium	262mg
Fiber	1g
Carbohydrates	72g
Sugar	56g
Vitamin A: 13% • Vitamin C: 4%	
Calcium: 10% • Iron: 8%	

INGREDIENTS

Topping
½ cup butter, fresh or powdered
1 cup brown sugar
1 can crushed pineapple, drained well

Cake
1⅓ cups flour
1 cup sugar
2 tablespoons egg crystals
⅓ cup butter powder
1½ teaspoons baking powder
½ teaspoon salt
2 tablespoons powdered milk
1¼ cups water at room temperature
1 teaspoon almond extract, optional

METHOD

1. *To prepare topping with real butter:* In a Dutch oven, reflector oven, or fry-bake pan, melt ½ cup butter and sprinkle brown sugar over top.

2. *To prepare topping with butter powder:* In a Dutch oven, reflector oven, or large fry-bake pan, bring ½ cup water to a boil. Pour butter powder and brown sugar into water then whisk steadily for 5 to 8 minutes until mixture begins to thicken into a caramel sauce.

3. Remove topping from heat but leave in baking pan.

4. Pour drained pineapple into caramel sauce and mix, spreading evenly along bottom of pan.

5. Pour 1¼ cup water into a zippered storage bag holding the dry cake ingredients.

6. Add 1 teaspoon almond extract to bag.

7. Close bag and massage thoroughly to mix all ingredients, rolling bag as needed to get into the corners.

8. Snip off a bottom corner of the bag then gently squeeze all batter out of the bag, directly on top of the pineapple-caramel mixture. Roll the bag like a toothpaste tube to get all batter and goodness out.

9. Bake for 40 to 50 minutes in Dutch oven, reflector oven, or fry-bake pan.

10. Test by inserting a fork or toothpick into the middle of the cake. It should come out clean when done.

11. Let cool for 5 minutes then loosen the edges of the cake with a knife.

12. Invert onto a plate, lid, or flexible cutting board. Leave pan or Dutch oven upside down for a few minutes so all the gooey goodness drains down onto the cake. Remove pan, and the golden-brown pineapple goodness will now be on top. Bon appétit!

Pineapple upside-down cake requires planning but is worth the wow factor. Photo: Sarah Hipple

Chocolate Raspberry Delight

Serves: 1 | **Weight: 0.36 lbs.** | V

This is a perfect pie-iron recipe (read more about them on page 27) that produces melty chocolate mixed with raspberry, all sealed up in a neat little package. If you don't have a pie iron, simply use your fry-bake pan and set a lid on top.

Servings	1
PER SERVING	
Calories	435
Fat	11g
Protein	9g
Sodium	436mg
Fiber	4g
Carbohydrates	74g
Sugar	33g
Vitamin A: 0% • Vitamin C: 3%	
Calcium: 4% • Iron: 14%	

INGREDIENTS

2 slices of leftover Bomber Bread, buttered
   (see page 120)
Pinch of cinnamon
1 teaspoon sugar
2 tablespoons chocolate-hazelnut spread (homemade or store-bought)
1 tablespoon raspberry jam

METHOD

1. Wipe out pie iron to make sure no savory flavors remain.

2. Butter bread then sprinkle buttered side with cinnamon and sugar.

3. Lay slice of bread butter-side down in pie iron. Top with hazelnut chocolate spread and raspberry jam.

4. Add second slice of bread, butter-side up.

5. Close lid over whole sandwich and toast in fire, 3 to 5 minutes per side.

COCOA VARIATIONS

Classic Cocoa

Serves: 4 | **Weight: 0.5 lbs** | V | GF | NF | ▲

What could be better after dinner in the backcountry than a steaming mug of homemade cocoa and a good book before bed? Not much! The variations below are easy to mix up at home then use like store-bought mix on the trail—except they're much tastier. You'll probably find yourself making them back in your everyday life, as well as on the trail.

Servings	4
PER SERVING	
Calories	147
Fat	3g
Protein	3g
Sodium	108mg
Fiber	2g
Carbohydrates	31g
Sugar	28g
Vitamin A: 2% • Vitamin C: 0%	
Calcium: 8% • Iron 4%	

INGREDIENTS
¼ cup cocoa powder
½ cup sugar
1 cup powdered milk
¼ teaspoon vanilla powder
⅛ teaspoon salt
4 cups water

METHOD
1. Whisk water into dry ingredients and heat to a simmer.
2. Alternatively, prepare single cups with a heaping ⅓ cup of powdered mix and a mug of hot water.

Mexican Cocoa

Serves: 4 | **Weight: 0.5 lbs.** | V GF NF

INGREDIENTS

Classic Cocoa, page 215
1 teaspoon cinnamon
4 cups water

METHOD

Add cinnamon to Classic Cocoa, page 215, and prepare as above.

Servings	4
PER SERVING	
Calories	**147**
Fat	3g
Protein	3g
Sodium	108mg
Fiber	2g
Carbohydrates	31g
Sugar	28g
Vitamin A: 2% • Vitamin C: 0%	
Calcium: 8% • Iron 4%	

Kids of all ages appreciate a mug of hot cocoa. Photo: Kyle LeBoeuf, Creative Commons on Flickr

Salted Caramel Cocoa

Serves: 4 | **Weight: 0.5 lbs.** | V | GF | NF

INGREDIENTS

Classic Cocoa, page 215
Unwrapped caramel candies
¼ teaspoon salt
4 cups hot water

METHOD

Unwrap candies and cover with hot water. Stir until caramels are fully dissolved. Stir powdered mix into hot water, as directed in Classic Cocoa, page 215.

Servings	4
PER SERVING	
Calories	33
Fat	0 g
Protein	0 g
Sodium	157 mg
Fiber	0 g
Carbohydrates	8 g
Sugar	7 g
Vitamin A: 0% • Vitamin C: 0%	
Calcium: 1% • Iron: 0%	

Winter Butter Cocoa

Serves: 4 | **Weight: 0.5 lbs.** | V | GF | NF

We know. It sounds crazy. But if you are out in the bitter cold, you will sing this drink's praises. The fat from the melted butter will keep you warm all through the night, and it tastes amazing!

INGREDIENTS

Classic Cocoa, page 215
4 cups water
1 tablespoon fresh butter

METHOD

Prepare Classic Cocoa, page 215, then plop in butter, stirring to melt for a salty-sweet, buttery treat.

Servings	4
PER SERVING	
Calories	201
Fat	12 g
Protein	0 g
Sodium	60 mg
Fiber	0 g
Carbohydrates	26 g
Sugar	26 g
Vitamin A: 7% • Vitamin C: 0%	
Calcium: 3% • Iron: 0%	

·············APPENDIX A:
BACKCOUNTRY RATIO GUIDE

Item	Dry Ingredient	Water	Notes
Coconut milk, powdered	1 part	2 parts	Mix well with cold water.
Couscous	1 part	1½ parts	Cover with water and bring to a boil. Remove from heat and let stand 5 minutes.
Egg crystals	2 parts	3 parts	Mix well with cold water before cooking.
Meat, dried	1 part	2 parts	Put dried meat in a bowl and cover with boiling water. Let stand 7 to 8 minutes, drain, and add to recipe.
Milk, powdered	1 part	4 parts	Mix well with cold water.
Potatoes, dehydrated	2 parts	3 parts	Mix flakes with boiling water and let stand 5 minutes.
Quinoa	1 part	2 parts	Rinse and drain. Put water and quinoa in a pot and bring to a boil. Reduce heat and simmer 15 minutes.
Rice, white	1 part	2 parts	Mix in pot, cover, bring to boil, lower to simmer, cook on low 20 minutes.
Rice, brown	1 part	2 parts	Mix in pot, cover, bring to boil, lower to simmer, cook on low 40 minutes.
Vegetables, dried	1 part	2 parts	Rehydrate vegetables by pouring boiling water over them and letting them stand 7 to 8 minutes. Or rehydrate by boiling along with whatever you're cooking.

The quickest way to build heat when you're cold: sugar and a hot beverage. Photo: Travis, Creative Commons on Flickr

Boiling is a reliable and inexpensive way to treat water before drinki

Photo: Michael Henry/AMC Photo Con

APPENDIX B: DRINKING WATER TREATMENT METHODS

The beautiful, clear streams and remote ponds of the mountains seem as pure as the snows from which they were formed. They look clean and clear and probably taste delicious! But every backcountry traveler should know that drinking this water without treating it brings the risk of ingesting micro-organisms that could lead to gastrointestinal discomfort, serious illness, and potential chronic concerns. Protozoan parasites, such as giardia and cryptosporidium, can cause acute gastrointestinal illness (diarrhea, cramp-ing, vomiting), and these parasites can occur in any untreated water. Water sources with heavy human impact can also contain viruses, such as hepatitis, or bacteria, such as E. coli.

For hikers who want to greatly lower the risk to themselves and their fel-low travelers, there are several good options for treating water and reducing the likelihood of a protozoan, bacterial, or viral infection. These water treat-ment options include boiling, filtering, ultraviolet radiation, chlorine-based chemicals, mixed oxidant systems, and iodine. All of these options remove or kill giardia and crypto, as well as any additional protozoa or bacteria in the water. Viruses, which are too small to be captured by filter systems, can be eliminated only with chemical treatment, boiling, or UV light.

Source: *AMC's Mountain Skills Manual* (AMC Books, 2017; outdoors.org/amcstore)

WHICH WATER TREATMENT METHOD IS RIGHT FOR YOU?		
Treatment Method	**Advantages**	**Disadvantages**
Boiling	▪ Rapidly treats larger quantities ▪ Reliable and inexpensive ▪ Works on all known pathogens	▪ Makes only hot water so requires ample cooling time for some uses ▪ Relies on stove or fire ▪ Requires fuel ▪ Imparts a taste
Pumping	▪ Leaves no taste ▪ Great for clean, clear sources	▪ Bulkier and heavier than other options ▪ Requires maintenance ▪ Requires effort and time ▪ Does not protect against viruses
Ultraviolet light	▪ Fast ▪ Easy to operate	▪ Battery dependent ▪ Must not be dropped or crushed in pack
Chlorine dioxide (chemical)	▪ Cost-effective, especially drops ▪ Easy to use ▪ Requires little trail time ▪ Mostly neutral taste impact	▪ Must have adequate supply for length of trip and size of group ▪ Requires 4 hours for complete confidence against cryptosporidium
Mixed-oxidant systems (chemical)	▪ As effective as all chlorine-based treatment options	▪ Battery dependent ▪ Requires rock salt ▪ Some aftertaste ▪ Requires 4 hours for complete confidence against cryptosporidium
Iodine (chemical)	▪ Small and light ▪ Easy to use ▪ Inexpensive	▪ Strong aftertaste ▪ Not safe for certain populations ▪ Not recommended for extended use ▪ Requires 4 hours for complete confidence against cryptosporidium
Straws	▪ Small and light	▪ Can take quite a bit of suction to get water through the straw

Source: *AMC's Mountain Skills Manual* (AMC Books, 2017; outdoors.org/amcstore)

DRINKING WATER TREATMENT METHODS FOR BACKCOUNTRY AND TRAVEL USE

Contaminant	Potential health effects from ingestion of water	Sources of contaminant in drinking water	Boiling[1]	Filtration[2]	Disinfection[3] Iodine* or Chlorine	Disinfection[3] Chlorine Dioxide	Combination of filtration and disinfection[4]
Protozoa Cryptosporidium	Gastrointestinal illness (e.g., diarrhea, vomiting, cramps)	Human and animal fecal waste	very high effectiveness	high effectiveness Absolute ≤ 1.0 micron filter (NSF Standard 53 or 58 rated "cyst reduction/removal" filter)	not effective	low to moderate effectiveness	very high effectiveness Absolute ≤ 1.0 micron filter (NSF Standard 53 or 58 rated "cyst reduction/removal" filter)
Protozoa Giardia intestinalis (a.k.a. Giardia lamblia)	Gastrointestinal illness (e.g., diarrhea, vomiting, cramps)	Human and animal fecal waste	very high effectiveness	high effectiveness Absolute ≤ 1.0 micron filter (NSF Standard 53 or 58 rated "cyst reduction/removal" filter)	low to moderate effectiveness	high effectiveness	very high effectiveness Absolute ≤ 1.0 micron filter (NSF Standard 53 or 58 rated "cyst reduction/removal" filter)
Bacteria (e.g., Campylobacter, Salmonella, Shigella, E. coli)	Gastrointestinal illness (e.g., diarrhea, vomiting, cramps)	Human and animal fecal waste	very high effectiveness	moderate effectiveness Absolute ≤ 0.3 micron filter	high effectiveness	high effectiveness	very high effectiveness Absolute ≤ 0.3 micron filter
Viruses (e.g., enterovirus, hepatitis A, norovirus, rotavirus)	Gastrointestinal illness (e.g., diarrhea, vomiting, cramps)	Human and animal fecal waste	very high effectiveness	not effective	high effectiveness	high effectiveness	very high effectiveness

[1]**Boiling** can be used as a pathogen reduction method that should kill all pathogens. Water should be brought to a rolling boil for 1 minute (at altitudes greater than 6,562 feet [>2,000 m], boil water for 3 minutes).

[2]**Filtration** can be used as a pathogen reduction method against most microorganisms, depending on the pore size of the filter, amount of the contaminant, and charge of the contaminant particle. Manufacturer's instructions must be followed. More information on selecting an appropriate water filter can be found at cdc.gov/crypto/factsheets/filters.html. Only filters that contain a chemical disinfectant matrix will be effective against some viruses.

[3]**Disinfection** can be used as a pathogen reduction method against microorganisms. However, contact time, disinfectant concentration, water temperature, water turbidity (cloudiness), water pH, and many other factors can impact the effectiveness of chemical disinfection. The length of time and concentration of disinfectant varies by manufacturer, and effectiveness of pathogen reduction depends on the product. Depending on these factors, 100% effectiveness may not be achieved. Manufacturer's instructions must be followed.

[4]If boiling water is not possible, a **combination of filtration and chemical disinfection** is the most effective pathogen reduction method in drinking water for backcountry or travel use. Manufacturer's instructions must be followed.

***Important:** Water that has been disinfected with iodine is NOT recommended for pregnant women, people with thyroid problems, those with known hypersensitivity to iodine, or continuous use for more than a few weeks at a time.

Other treatment methods can be effective against some of the above pathogens:

Ultraviolet Light (UV Light) can be used as a pathogen reduction method against some microorganisms. The technology requires effective prefiltering due to its dependence on low water turbidity (cloudiness), the correct power delivery, and correct contact times to achieve maximum pathogen reduction. UV might be an effective method for pathogen reduction in untreated or poorly treated water; there is a lack of independent testing available on specific systems. Manufacturer's instructions must be followed.

MIOX® systems use a salt solution to create mixed oxidants, primarily chlorine. As a result, refer to the category above for chlorine disinfection. Manufacturer's instructions must be followed.

In addition to using the appropriate drinking water treatment methods listed above, you can also protect yourself and others from waterborne illness by **burying human waste** 8 inches deep and at least 200 feet away from natural waters and **practicing good personal hygiene** (wash hands before handling food, eating, and after using the toilet).

Source: CDC Fact Sheet for Healthy Drinking Water, cdc.gov/healthywater.

INDEX

A
all-purpose mixes, 16
animal safety, 41–43

B
bacon, precooked, 21
bacon dishes. See sausage/bacon dishes
bear considerations, 33
beef dishes
  beef jerkies, 89–91
  Beef Stroganoff, 147
  Creamed Chipped Beef, 194
  Frozen Steaks Alfresco, 201
  Unstuffed Peppers with Beef, 200
breads and wraps, 120–131
  Bannock, 123
  Basic Calzones, 126
  Basic Pizza, 125–126
  Burritos, 130
  Cornbread, 122
  Cozy Pigs, 131
  Ethan's Bomber Bread, 120–121
  Pozole Pie, 127–128
  Quesadillas, 128–129
breakfast bars, 55
  granola bars, 108–113
breakfast dishes, 50–81
  breakfast bars, 55
  egg dishes, 64–71
  granola, 50–55
  muffins, 56–60
  oatmeal, 76–77
  pancakes, 61–62
  potato/grain dishes, 72–77
  sweet treats, 78–81

C
cakes, savory, 155–157
  Cheesy Potato Cakes, 155
  Veggie Potato Cakes, 156–157
calorie needs, 2

campfires, cooking over, 36–37
camp kitchen, 33
caramel rolls, 80–81
carbohydrates, 2–4
chicken dishes
  Buffalo Mac and Cheese, 154
  Chicken and Bacon Cheesy Pasta, 136
  Chicken and Veggie Curry, 182
  Chicken Cheesy Rice, 159
  Chicken Tikka Masala, 185
  Curried Quinoa with Chicken, 178
  One-Pot Deconstructed Enchilada, 189
  Pad Thai, 148
  Quick Chicken and Rice Stew, 186
  Stuffing with Chicken and Cranberries, 171
  Tortilla Soup, 190
cocoa drinks, 215–217
coffee, 48–49
coffee cake, 78–79
condiments, 21–23
cornstarch, 20
corn syrup, 20–21
couscous dishes, 163–168
  Couscous with Salmon, Tomatoes, and Zucchini, 167
  Curried Broccoli Couscous, 164
  Herbed Israeli Couscous, 163
  Moroccan Couscous, 166
  Steph'z Southwestern "Couz-Couz," 168
curries, stews, and soups, 182–193
  Broccoli and Cheddar Soup, 191
  Chicken and Veggie Curry, 182
  Chicken Tikka Masala, 185
  Chili con Carne, 188–189
  Cuban Black Bean Soup, 192
  Indonesian Sweet Potato and Cabbage Stew, 186
  Lentil Soup, 193
  One-Pot Deconstructed Enchilada, 189

Quick Chicken and Rice Stew, 186
Thai Coconut Curry, 184
Tortilla Soup, 190

D

dairy, 5–6
dehydrating foods, 16–19
desserts. See sweet dishes
dinners
  breads and wraps, 120–131
  curries, stews, and soups, 182–193
  other grains and carbs, 163–181
  other meat and fish meals, 194–201
  pastas, 132–154
  rice dishes, 157–162
  sauces, dried, 116–118
  savory cakes, 155–157
dishwashing, 44
drinks
  Classic Cocoa, 215
  Mexican Cocoa, 216
  Salted Caramel Cocoa, 217
  Winter Butter Cocoa, 217
dutch ovens, 39–40

E

egg dishes, 64–71
  Basic Egg Scramble, 64–65
  Breakfast Burritos, 70
  Denver Scramble, 66
  Hash Brown and Bacon Scramble,
    68–69
  Huevos Rancheros, 67
  Omelet in a Bag, 71
  Spinach, Mushroom, and Bacon
    Scramble, 69

F

falafel, 180
fats, 6
fiber, 4
fish, cooking of, 41
fish dishes
  Couscous with Salmon, Tomatoes and
    Zucchini, 167
  Garlic and Thyme Fish on a Stick, 196
  Lemon Butter Trout, 195
  Salmon Fried Rice, 158–159

Trout Picatta, 198
Tuna Pea Wiggle, 146
flavor, 6–7
fruit leathers, 86–88
  Basic Fruit Leather, 86
  Mixed Berry Fruit Leather, 88
  Strawberry Fruit Leather, 88
  Sweet and Spicy Mango Fruit Leather,
    87
fry-bake pans, 40–41

G

gear, essential, 23–25
GORP, 97
grains, 3
granola, 50–54
  Almond Sesame Mango Granola, 52
  Basic Granola, 50
  Coconut Cashew Granola, 51
  Cranberry Nut Granola, 52
  Dark Chocolate Coconut Granola, 54
  Pistachio Apricot Granola, 53
granola bars, 108–113
  Blueberry Granola Bars with Vanilla
    Icing, 111–112
  Cherry Choco-Nut Granola Bars, 109
  Chocolate Peanut Butter Granola
    Bars, 110
  Double Chocolate Granola Bars, 108
  Ski Bars, 113

H

hanging of food, 42–43
Hobo Dinner, 199–200
Hummus, 105–106

I

ingredients, choosing of, 12–14

J

jerkies, 89–92
  Basic Beef Jerky, 89
  Honey Barbecue Beef Jerky, 90
  Malaysian Pork Jerky (Bak Kwa), 92
  Peppered Beef Jerky, 91
  Teriyaki Beef Jerky, 90

L

Leave No Trace principles, 34
lunches/snacks, 86–113
  fruit leathers, 86–88
  granola bars, 108–113
  jerkies, 89–92
  nuts/nut butters, 93–100
  recommended quantities, 83
  smorgasbord combos, 84–85
  veggie nibbles and spreads, 101–107

M

macaroni and cheese recipes, 152–154
meal-planning grid, 11–12
muffins, 56–60
  Basic Skillet Muffins, 56–57
  Blueberry Skillet Muffins, 59
  Cranberry Orange Skillet Muffins, 60
  Donut Skillet Muffins, 58
  Morning Glory Skillet Muffins, 60

N

nutrition, 1–6
nuts/nut butters, 93–100
  Cashew Butter, 99
  Chipotle Honey Roasted Peanuts, 94
  Chocolate Hazelnut Heaven, 100
  Cinnamon-Spiced Pecans, 96
  Curried Almonds, 95
  Fruits and Nuts Trail Mix, 98
  Good Old Raisins and Peanuts (GORP), 97
  Sweet and Spicy Rosemary Cashews, 93
  Tropical Trail Mix, 97

O

Oatmeal, 76–77

P

packing of food, 28–29
paddling extras, 27
pancakes, 61–62
pastas, 132–154
  Beef Stroganoff, 147
  Cauliflower Pine Nut Pasta, 134

Chicken and Bacon Cheesy Pasta, 136
Chili Mac, 145
Fettuccine Alfredo, 141
5-Minute Gado Gado, 133
Gado Gado Noodles in Peanut Sauce, 132
Gnocchi with Browned Butter and Sage, 142
lasagna, baked, 149–150
lasagna, deconstructed, 151
macaroni and cheese, bacon and kale, 154
macaroni and cheese, basic, 152
macaroni and cheese, Buffalo, 154
Mushroom Rigatoni, 140
Pad Thai, 148
Penne with Squash, Tomatoes, and Basil, 138
Pesto Pasta with Sun-Dried Tomatoes and Pine Nuts, 143
Pesto Pasta with Veggies, 144
Tortellini Carbonara, 137
Tuna Pea Wiggle, 146
pie irons, 27
pizza-type dishes, 125–128
polenta dishes, 169–170
  Fried Polenta Cakes with Beans and Salsa, 170
  Polenta Pizza, 169
potato/grain dishes, 72–77
  Backcountry Home Fries, 72–73
  Baked Potatoes, 181
  Fried Bagels, 73
  Fried PB&J Pita, 74
  Tasha's Breakfast Couscous, 75
proteins, 4–5

Q

quinoa dishes, 173–179
  Almond Sesame Quinoa, 176
  "Caretaker's Dream" Stir-Fry, 179
  Cheesy Broccoli, Sausage, and Quinoa, 173
  Cheesy Quinoa with Sweet Potato, Black Beans, and Corn, 177
  Curried Quinoa with Chicken, 178
  Quinoa with Pistachios and Dried Cherries, 174

R

ratio guide, 219
reflector ovens, 38–39
rehydration, 45
repackaging, 14–16
resupplying, 29–30
rice dishes, 157–162
    Chicken Cheesy Rice, 159
    Coconut Rice, 161
    Mexican Rice, 162
    Orange Ginger Rice, 160
    Salmon Fried Rice, 158–159
    Sausage and Rice, 157

S

safety considerations, 34–36
sauces, dried
    Alfredo Sauce, 116
    Marinara Sauce, 117
    Pesto Sauce, 118
sausage/bacon dishes
    Bacon and Kale Mac and Cheese, 154
    Cheesy Broccoli, Sausage, and
        Quinoa, 173
    Chicken and Bacon Cheesy Pasta, 136
    Cuban Black Bean Soup, 192
    Hash Brown and Bacon Scramble,
        68–69
    Sausage and Rice, 157
    Spinach, Mushroom, and Bacon
        Scramble, 69
    Stuffing and Sausage, 172
    Tortellini Carbonara, 137
smorgasbord combos
    Cheddar and Slivered Garlic Lunch
        Combo, 84
    Sardines, Avocado, and Hardtack
        Lunch Combo, 85
snacks. See lunches/snacks
soups. See curries, stews, and soups
special diets, 7–9
spice kits, 21
spreads. See veggie nibbles and spreads
starches, 2–3
stews. See curries, stews, and soups
stoves, 26–27

stuffings, 171–172
    Stuffing and Sausage, 172
    Stuffing with Chicken and
        Cranberries, 171
sugar, 3–4
sweet dishes
    Caramel Corn, 210
    caramel rolls, See Sarah's Super-
        Sticky Caramel Rolls, 80–81
    Chocolate Hazelnut Heaven, 100
    Chocolate Raspberry Delight, 214
    coffee cake, See Dottie's Downhome
        Coffee Cake, 78–79
    granola bars, 108–113
    No-Bake Cookies, 209
    Oatmeal Chocolate Peanut Butter
        Cookies, 207
    Peanut Butter Squares, 206
    Pineapple Upside-Down Cake,
        212–213
    Scotch-a-Roos, 204
    Sopapillas, 211
    Trail Mix Cookies, 205

T

Taco Seasoning, 119
trail mixes, 97–98
    Trail Mix Cookies, 205

V

vegetables, 5
veggie nibbles and spreads, 101–107
    Ants on a Log, 101
    Banana Boat, 102
    Black Bean Spread, 107
    Buffalo Cauliflower "Popcorn," 104
    Hummus, 105
    Peanut Butter-Filled Dates, 103
    White Bean Spread, 107

W

water purification, 43, 221–223

NOTES

APPALACHIAN MOUNTAIN CLUB

At AMC, connecting you to the freedom and exhilaration of the outdoors is our calling. We help people of all ages and abilities to explore and develop a deep appreciation of the natural world.

AMC helps you get outdoors on your own, with family and friends, and through activities close to home and beyond. With chapters from Maine to Washington, D.C., including groups in Boston, New York City, and Philadelphia, you can enjoy activities like hiking, paddling, cycling, and skiing, and learn new outdoor skills. We offer advice, guidebooks, maps, and unique lodges and huts to inspire your next outing. You will also have the opportunity to support conservation advocacy and research, youth programming, and caring for 1,800 miles of trails.

We invite you to join us in the outdoors.

YOUR CONNECTION
TO THE OUTDOORS

White Mountain Guide, 30th Edition

Compiled and Edited by Steven D. Smith

Now in print for 110 years, AMC's comprehensive *White Mountain Guide* remains hikers' most trusted resource for the White Mountain National Forest and surrounding regions. New in this thoroughly updated 30th edition are at-a-glance icons for suggested hikes and easier-to-follow statistics for all 500-plus trails. Includes a set of six pull-out maps.

$24.95 • 978-1-934028-85-8

AMC's Mountain Skills Manual

Christian Bisson and Jamie Hannon

This comprehensive guide tackles the essential skills every hiker should master. Beginners will learn hiking basics such as gear, navigation, safety, and stewardship. More experienced readers can hone backpacking skills, including trip planning, efficient packing, and advanced wilderness ethics. All readers will map new adventures, perfect their pace, or simply plan a fun weekend of camping and day-hikes.

$21.95 • 978-1-62842-025-8

AMC's Best Backpacking in New England

Matt Heid

Explore the region's wildest trails in 37 overnight trips, from maritime delights of Cape Cod's Sandy Neck and Maine's Cutler Coast, to the wild forests of Monroe State Forest in Massachusetts and Vermont's Glastenbury Mountain Wilderness, to classic backpacking pilgrimages through the 100-Mile Wilderness and across the Presidential Range.

$19.95 • 978-1-934028-90-2

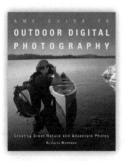

AMC Guide to Outdoor Digital Photography

Jerry Monkman

Explore the process of outdoor photography—from packing and taking care of gear, to setting up and taking great shots, to processing photos in the digital darkroom. Full-color photographs pair with seasoned tips and advice to comprise a must-have guide for anyone interested in outdoor nature and adventure photography.

$19.95 • 978-1-934028-50-6

Find print and ebook versions of these and other AMC titles at outdoors.org/amcstore or call 800-262-4455. AMC Books are also available at bookstores, outdoor retailers, and online marketplaces.